# LACROSSE ESSENTIALS

## Jack B. Kaley
## Rich Donovan

**Human Kinetics**

**Library of Congress Cataloging-in-Publication Data**

Kaley, Jack B.
  Lacrosse essentials / Jack B. Kaley, Rich Donovan.
     pages cm
1. Lacrosse--Training.  I. Donovan, Rich. II. Title.
  GV989.15.K35 2015
  796.34'7--dc23

                          2014046742

ISBN: 978-1-4504-0215-6 (print)

The web addresses cited in this text were current as of December 2014 unless otherwise noted.

**Acquisitions Editor:** Justin Klug; **Developmental Editor:** Anne Hall; **Managing Editor:** Elizabeth Evans; **Copyeditor:** Annette Pierce; **Permissions Manager:** Martha Gullo; **Graphic Designer:** Dawn Sills; **Cover Designer:** Keith Blomberg; **Photograph (cover):** © FOTOSEARCH RM/age fotostock; **Photographs (interior):** Neil Bernstein; **Visual Production Assistant:** Joyce Brumfield; **Photo Production Manager:** Jason Allen; **Art Manager:** Kelly Hendren; **Associate Art Manager:** Alan L. Wilborn; **Illustrations:** © Human Kinetics; **Printer:** Versa Press

We thank the New York Institute of Technology in Old Westbury, New York, for assistance in providing the location for the photo shoot for this book.

Human Kinetics books are available at special discounts for bulk purchase. Special editions or book excerpts can also be created to specification. For details, contact the Special Sales Manager at Human Kinetics.

Printed in the United States of America        10  9  8  7  6  5  4  3  2  1

The paper in this book is certified under a sustainable forestry program.

**Human Kinetics**
Website: www.HumanKinetics.com

*United States:* Human Kinetics
P.O. Box 5076
Champaign, IL 61825-5076
800-747-4457
e-mail: humank@hkusa.com

*Canada:* Human Kinetics
475 Devonshire Road Unit 100
Windsor, ON N8Y 2L5
800-465-7301 (in Canada only)
e-mail: info@hkcanada.com

*Europe:* Human Kinetics
107 Bradford Road
Stanningley
Leeds LS28 6AT, United Kingdom
+44 (0) 113 255 5665
e-mail: hk@hkeurope.com

*Australia:* Human Kinetics
57A Price Avenue
Lower Mitcham, South Australia 5062
08 8372 0999
e-mail: info@hkaustralia.com

*New Zealand:* Human Kinetics
P.O. Box 80
Torrens Park, South Australia 5062
0800 222 062
e-mail: info@hknewzealand.com

E5305

For my darling wife, Monika, whose support,
devotion, and encouragement made this a reality,
and for my daughter, Amanda, for her love
and the joy she has given me.
*Jack Kaley*

For my wife, Cheryl, with gratitude for the unconditional
love you've given our family every day, your support
inspired me to pursue my coaching dreams at every
level of lacrosse; for Caitlin and Michael, my happiest
moments in life have been as your father.
*Rich Donovan*

# Contents

# Acknowledgments

I would like to acknowledge my coaches, Bill Ritch and Howdy Myers, who instilled in me the fundamentals, love, and devotion to the game; Alan Lowe, Bob Cook, Bruce Casagrande, Bob Calabretta, George Searing, Tim Tuttle, Chris Bergerson, Rich Donovan, and Bill Dunn, and all my other assistant coaches who have been such a vital part of our success over the years. Special thanks go to our parents, Kathy Spruyt, Kathy Broschart, Diane Cullin, Trudy Hennessey, Bob Hunter, Frank D'Andrea, John Sullivan, and Bob Marr for our pasta dinners. A special thanks to Tim Gruenke, who gave both Rich and me the opportunity to coach Team Germany. Finally, to all my players, for their dedication and work ethic who made our success possible.

*Jack Kaley*

I am grateful for the many teammates, coaches, officials, parents, friends, and student athletes who have touched my life through our interaction in the sport of lacrosse. Many thanks to my parents, James and Catherine Donovan; Michael Lettera and Joe Cavallo, exemplary teammates in sports and life; Stan Sheie, my first coach; Tom Fitzpatrick, for his leadership; Jack Kaley, who inspired me as a player and coach; Dick Garber and Greg Cannella, for their commitment to a tradition of excellence; Bob Shillinglaw and Dave Slafkosky, for sharing their friendship, passion, and expertise; Ernie Olson, Wayne Ament, and Matt Cady, for their support; Michael Magee, for his guidance; Ed Schreiber, for his integrity; Dan Nolan, for his courage; and Bill Vita, for his wisdom.

*Rich Donovan*

# Key to Diagrams

⊗ ——————— Ball carrier

○ ——————— Ball

● ——————— Starting ball

D ——————— Defenseman

X ——————— Defensive midfielder

O ——————— Offensive player

A ——————— Attackman

C ——————— Creaseman

W ——————— Wingman

M ——————— Offensive midfielder

P ——————— Player

G ——————— Goalie

LSM ——————— Long-stick midfielder

SS ——————— Short-stick midfielder

GLE ——————— Goal line extended

⟶ ——————— Cut movement

- - -⟶ ——————— Ball movement; pass

——⊣ ——————— Pick movement

〰⟶ ——————— Rotation movement

·····⟶ ——————— Defense movement

■ ——————— Coach

△ ——————— Cone

⧌ ——————— Goal

# CHAPTER 1

# The Game of Lacrosse

Lacrosse is a game played between two teams of at least 10 players. All teams consist of three attackmen, three midfielders, three defensemen, and one goalie. Although teams might use other positions, these four are the most universally used. Specialty positions largely depend on the coach's philosophy or coaching style. For example, a coach might designate a face-off specialist or a short-stick defensive midfielder. Not every team will use specialty roles, but it's not uncommon.

## MAIN POSITIONS

Each position serves a specific role within the team's system of play. The following are the most common responsibilities of each of the four main positions.

### Attack

As your primary offensive players, the main role for an attack player is to score goals; however, their responsibilities stretch beyond scoring. On shots that do not score, the attackmen's job is to regain possession of the ball and prevent the defense from clearing the ball. Loose balls occur frequently throughout a game. Because they can happen at any point, the attack players must be aware of the ball's location at all times to avoid losing possession.

### Defense

The defenders have one of the most difficult tasks in the game. Their main responsibility is to stop the opponent from scoring. Most defenders use sticks that have longer handles. This allows them to cover a greater area of the field. Playing defense is a difficult and often a dangerous role. Defenders often find themselves in the line of a shot taken by the other team. Being unaware of their surroundings or where the ball is can result in being hit by a shot, so they must constantly swivel their head back and forth and be ready to defend properly.

## Midfield

Midfielders play both sides of the field. They must possess strong offensive skills but also be able to turn around and defend against the opposition. These players are typically the best all-around athletes and have excellent stamina. Although these players are in the game for only short periods, they must be able to play at full speed every second they're on the field.

## Goal

The role of the goalie is somewhat obvious: to stop shots from going into the net. But the goalie's responsibility doesn't end there. He is responsible for clearing the ball after making a save and communicating to his teammates throughout an opponent's possession.

# FIELD OF PLAY

Depending on the level of competition, the field dimensions vary. For high school levels and above, the field is 110 yards long and 60 yards wide. Youth lacrosse field dimensions vary significantly depending on where the game is played. Often the field's length is considerably shorter because of space restrictions and to allow players to learn the game without having to cover substantial distances (see figure 1.1).

## Crossfield Lines: Center Line, Goal Line Extended, and End Line

Specific lines on the field play important roles during the game. The center line, or midline, divides the field into two halves: the defensive side and the offensive side. Similar to ice hockey players, all lacrosse players are permitted to use the full field. Although players can use the entire field, the rules require that four players always be on the defensive side of the midline and three players always be on the offensive side of the midline. Also, face-offs take place at the midpoint of this center line.

The goal line extended is an imaginary line extending from the goal line to the sidelines. Both the offensive and defensive teams use this imaginary line. Defensemen are taught to play top side of this line and to try to prevent the attackmen from penetrating above it. Some offensive teams use

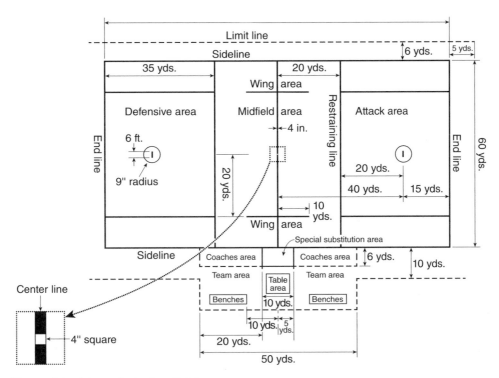

**Figure 1.1**   Map of playing field.

this line to set up feeds and to time their cuts. The end line marks the back edge of the playing field.

## Playing Zones

In addition to the offensive and defensive halves, the field is further defined by the restraining lines in each half of the field, and the playing zones are within each area.

Within each zone are lines marking specific areas, including the offensive area, defensive area, and wing area. Each of these zones serves a specific purpose to the game.

### Wing Area

The wing area is designated by a line parallel to the sideline and 20 yards from the face-off X on both sides of the field. On face-offs, the wingmen line up behind this line. This line extends 10 yards in either direction from the midline. The wingmen may position themselves anywhere in the wing area so long as they are behind the wing line. The wingmen normally position themselves where the face-off man anticipates the ball will wind up. Normally, one wingman takes an offensive position, meaning the side where he thinks the face-off man will position the ball, and the other takes a defensive position in case the opposing creaseman wins the face-off.

## Offensive Area

The offensive area is marked by a solid line 20 yards above the goal line extended. It extends 20 yards in both directions from the center of the field and from this point extends to the back end line parallel to the sidelines. The offensive area is 40 yards wide and 35 yards deep.

## Defensive Area

The defensive area is the same as the offensive area, but on the defensive half of the field. Lanes are the passing areas used by the offensive and defensive players. The ball travels through these areas. Defenses use the top of the box as a guide for when to pick up and apply pressure. Defenses using zones also use the top of the box to help them recognize the seams of the zone. These lines are important for both offensive and defensive teams when executing their riding and clearing patterns.

# EQUIPMENT

Goals are 6 feet wide and 6 feet high and are constructed of 1.5-inch-diameter pipe that is painted orange. Each goal, or cage, is fitted with a pyramid-shaped net that extends 7 feet behind the center of the cage and is fastened to the ground. Although nets may be of any solid color, they are usually white. The ball is made of solid rubber and can be white, yellow, or orange and must meet the National Operating Committee on Standards for Athletic Equipment (NOCSAE).

Three sticks are used in lacrosse. The attack stick used by both attackmen and midfielders can be 40 to 42 inches long. The short stick gives offensive players a better opportunity to protect the stick as well as improve stick work. Defensemen use a stick that is 52 to 72 inches long. This extra length gives defensemen a better opportunity to stick-check their opponents and to cut off passing lanes. The defensive stick can be up to 10 inches wide; whereas, the offensive player's stick can be as narrow as 6.5 inches. These are inside measurements at the widest point. The length of the head is a minimum of 10 inches from the outside edge of the head to the beginning of the throat of the stick. Ball stops are not required, but if one is used, it must be perpendicular to the handle of the stick and wide enough to permit the ball to rest loosely on the stop. The goalie's stick is 40 to 72 inches long. The head of the stick should be no more than 16.5 inches long and 10 to 12 inches wide.

The following protective equipment is mandatory for each player. It should be manufactured professionally and meet NOCSAE standards:

1. Helmet with a chin pad and chin strap
2. Face mask

3. A properly fitted tooth and mouth protector
4. Gloves, arm pads, and shoulder pads
5. Throat protector and chest protector for goalies

Shoes may be canvas, leather, or synthetic and may or may not have cleats. Uniform jerseys and shorts must be of the same color. The size of the numbers on the front of the jersey depends on the level of the team. In high school, the front number must be at least 8 inches tall. In college, the front number must be 10 inches. In both cases, the back number must be at least 12 inches tall, and the front and back numbers should be centered vertically.

The head coach is responsible for certifying with the referee before the game that all players are properly equipped and that the equipment is worn properly. He also notifies the officials of the captains and the in-home player at this time. The first starting attackman listed in the official scorebook lineup is the in-home player. The in-home player is the first player listed in the scorebook who will serve any team penalty.

## STARTING THE GAME

About 5 minutes before the game is scheduled to begin, the captains for both teams meet the referees at the center of the field. At this time, the referees address the expectations of good sportsmanship, and a coin toss determines who will defend which goal in the first quarter. Before the opening face-off, the referee lines up the players facing each other at the center of the field, with their left sides to the goal they are defending. He explains special ground rules should they exist.

Play starts at the beginning of each quarter and after every goal with a face-off. The official places the ball at the center face-off X. The face-off men line up at the X, and the wingmen line up in the wing areas at the same time. On the face-off, the stick and ball are positioned 4 inches from each other at the center stripe.

The sticks must be on the ground along the center line and parallel to each other but not touching the ball. Once the official signals set, both players must remain motionless until the whistle starts play. At the sound of the whistle, each player attempts to control the movement of the ball with his stick. The face-off man may not touch the ball with his gloves at any time during this maneuver. At the sound of the whistle, the two face-off men and the four wingmen are free to play the ball. The attackmen and defensemen must stay in their designated areas until a player from either team has gained possession of the ball, the ball goes out of bounds, or the ball crosses into their area.

If the team has one or more players out of the game on a penalty going into a face-off situation, that team is allowed to bring up an attackman to play the wing area on the offensive side of the field. During the face-off, the attackman is free to leave the wing area to help gain possession of the ball. This team must obey the provisions of the offside rule. For example, if this team loses possession of the ball on that face-off, the attackman must remain back in his offensive half of the field.

# GAME SEQUENCE

Play will stop any time the ball is out of bounds. The ball is out of bounds when a player in possession steps on or beyond the boundary line. That player loses possession and the ball is awarded to the nearest player of the opposing team. The ball is put into play immediately at the point where it went out of bounds. On a restart, the opposing team must give the player with possession of the ball a minimum of 5 yards. On a shot or a deflected shot at the goal, the ball is awarded to the nearest player to the spot where the ball went out of bounds. In an out-of-bounds situation, the ball is awarded to the team opposing the player who last touched the ball. If the ball goes out of bounds directly from the face-off and neither player had control of the ball, it will be refaced. Anytime the officials cannot determine which team should be awarded the ball, possession alternates. Alternating possession is determined by a pregame coin flip.

A goal is scored when the ball passes from the front of the goal and breaks the imaginary plane formed by the rear edges of the goalposts. A goal may be disallowed under the following conditions:

1. After the horn sounds to end a period
2. When a player of the attacking team is in the crease area
3. When the attacking team is offsides
4. When one of the officials has sounded the whistle for any reason, even if by mistake
5. If the head comes off the stick on a shot
6. When there is a foul by the scoring team
7. If a player from the attacking team was released early from the penalty box
8. When the scoring player's stick is found to be illegal or he adjusts his stick in any way after the official asks for it
9. If a teammate is in the crease or interferes with the goalie while his teammate is in the act of shooting
10. When an official recognizes a time-out from the team in possession of the ball, regardless of whether the official has had time to blow the whistle
11. If an attacking player's momentum carries him into the crease area before or after the ball is in the goal

In high school play, the rules require the clearing team to advance the ball over the center line within 20 seconds. (Normally, the clearing team gains possession of the ball and moves it from its defensive half of the field to its offensive half of the field.) Failure to do so results in a turnover, with the opposing team getting possession of the ball. Once the 20-second count has started, it remains in effect until the clearing team clears the ball over the midline, a loose ball breaks the plane of the midline, or officials sound the whistle to stop play for any reason. Once the team with possession crosses the midfield line, it has 10 seconds to get the ball into its offensive zone. Once inside the offensive zone, players may bring the ball outside the offensive area as often as they like until the referee signals to keep it in. Once they have been warned by the officials, they have a new 10-second count to get the ball into the offensive area and now must keep it in the area. If the ball comes out of the area for any reason, it results in a turnover.

Teams exchange goals at the end of each quarter. In the event of a tie, a coin toss decides which goal will be defended. All sudden-victory overtime periods last 4 minutes or until a goal is scored. Each team receives one time-out per period. The team that calls a time-out has the discretion to use the full time-out (1 minute, 40 seconds) or less. For example, if a team calls a time-out and uses just 30 seconds of it, the officials must notify the other team that the time-out is over and must restart the game within 20 seconds. Restarts following a time-out occur at the spot closest to where the ball was when the time-out whistle was blown. If the ball was in the goal area when play was suspended, play is restarted outside the goal area nearest the spot where the ball was at the time of the whistle.

# SUBSTITUTION

Substitution may take place any time play has been suspended by an official or after a goal, a time-serving penalty has expired, or a time-out is called. Any time the ball goes out of bounds on the sidelines, a coach may call for a horn to request a substitution. When the ball goes out at the end line, no substitution is permitted. Substitutions may take place at any time while the game is in progress so long as the substituting player does not enter the field until the player he's replacing has exited. The substituting players must meet the onside rules.

# PERMISSIBLE CHECKS AND SCREENS

Some important permissible aspects of the game are subject to interpretation by the officials. Coaches and players must understand what is permitted and what is not.

- Stick checking your opponent's stick with your own stick is legal when your opponent has possession of the ball or is within 5 yards of a loose ball.

- Body checking is a check from the front or side above the waist and below the neck is a legal body check when the player has possession or is within 5 yards of a loose ball.
- Picking is the stationary screening of an opponent. It is legal so long as the offensive man screening is motionless before contact is made.

# PERSONAL FOULS

Personal fouls include slashing, illegal body checking, tripping, crosschecking, unnecessary roughness, unsportsmanlike conduct, and use of an illegal stick. The penalty for a personal foul is suspension from the game for 1 to 3 minutes, depending on the official's judgment of the severity and perceived intent of the foul. The ball is awarded to the team that was fouled. This results in an extra-man opportunity for the team that was fouled. A man-down situation for the team that was penalized occurs for the duration of the penalty.

The following are personal fouls listed in approximate order of the frequency that an official calls them during a game.

## Slashing

This penalty is the one most often called. It's a result of an uncontrolled check that misses the intended target: the glove or stick. A check that comes into contact with the body or head of the ball carrier is also a slash. Quite often a stick check that hits the arm or body of the offensive player can be deemed a slash. In some situations, what started as a legal check comes into contact with the offensive player. In this situation, it is up to the official whether to call a slashing foul or not. There is not much value in teaching the slap check because the official will often call it a slash. Checks that are just as effective and less likely to end in a penalty are the poke check and the lift check. These legal checks are explained in chapter 6.

## Tripping

Tripping happens when a player uses any part of his body or stick to trip an opponent. It is normally unintentional and happens when two or more players compete for a loose ball.

## Illegal Body Check

Although body checking is legal, it is rarely allowed in today's game. More often than not it results in one of many infractions, such as hitting above the shoulder, following through with the shaft of the stick, or even hitting the player with unnecessary roughness. Therefore limit use of body checking. The only time to use it is when a player makes the second-slide attempt to stop the offensive player from penetrating the defense. In this situation, execute a stuff, which is similar to taking a charge in basketball, but in lacrosse you don't have to remain stationary to execute a stuff.

## Cross Checking

This occurs when a player checks, holds, or pushes an opponent in the back or side with the shaft of his stick. It is illegal to check an opponent with the handle of a stick that is between both hands.

## Unnecessary Roughness

Unnecessary roughness is called when an infraction of the rules against holding, pushing, or hitting is excessively violent. It also includes running into a player setting a pick deliberately and with violent intent.

## Unsportsmanlike Conduct

This foul can be given to any team member or anyone officially connected with the team for the following infractions: arguing excessively over an official's call, using threatening or obscene language or gestures during a ball game, or repeatedly committing the same technical foul (for example, questioning an official's call).Unsportsmanlike conduct can also be called when a player deliberately fails to comply with the rules for entering the field of play. Finally, any player who commits five personal fouls will be disqualified from the game.

## Ejection From the Game

Any member of the team or anyone officially connected with the team may be ejected for fighting; leaving the bench on an altercation; using tobacco; committing a second, nonreleasable, unsportsmanlike penalty; or performing an action deemed as misconduct by the officials. A nonreleasable penalty is a penalty that is served for the full length of time, regardless of how many goals are scored.

# TECHNICAL FOULS

Technical fouls are less serious than personal or ejection fouls. Technical fouls incur either a 30-second penalty or loss of possession of the ball if your team had possession at the time the foul was committed. The ball is awarded to the other team at the spot where the foul was committed. The following technical fouls are listed in the approximate order of the frequency that an official calls them during a game.

## Holding

This penalty is called when a player impedes the movement of the opponent's stick. The defensive player may not use his stick to hold an opponent nor can he check the stick of an opponent if he doesn't have the ball. He cannot use his stick or freehand to hold an opponent. A defensive player is permitted to hold his stick on the offensive stick but is not permitted to prevent the free movement of the offensive player's stick. It is up to the official to determine whether the defensive player is preventing the free movement of the offensive player's stick. Because this is a gray area and up to the judgment of the official, this foul is called frequently.

## Offside

An offside call is made when a team is in excess of the allotted number of players on the offensive or defensive half of the field. Teams are limited to four players on the defensive half and three players on the offensive half of the field. These numbers are constant, regardless of position.

## Interference

A player should not interfere with the free movement of an opponent unless he is the ball carrier or he is within 5 yards of the ball. This rule protects the offensive player.

## Illegal Offensive Screening (Setting Picks)

No offensive player shall move into or make contact with a defensive player for the purpose of denying that player access to the man he is guarding. The offensive player may not move or use his stick to impede the free movement of a defensive player. All screens (picks) by offensive players must be motionless before the contact occurs. Because this is a judgment call by the official, the burden of responsibility is on the offensive player, who must remain stationary when setting the screen.

## Crease Violations

Interference with the goalie while he and the ball are in the crease, whether or not he has possession of the ball, is a play-on situation. The crease area is the space utilized by the goalie. A play-on situation is when the goalie has possession and is allowed to run the ball out of the crease or successfully complete an outlet pass. If he does not exercise those options, the whistle sounds and his team gets possession of the ball at the offensive side of the field at the center X. If the ball is loose in the crease and the goalie gains possession after the play-on signal has been given, the play is over and the defensive team regains possession at the midfield X.

If the defensive team has possession of the ball in a play-on situation, the referee will allow the team to continue play so long as it has possession and is advancing the ball to the opponent's goal. The whistle will be sounded after possession has been lost, a shot has been taken, or a goal has been scored. The offending team will then serve its penalty. The exception is if the penalty was a technical and a goal had been scored. In that situation, the goal counts and the technical is wiped out. If no goal was scored, the team committing the penalty serves time depending on whether the foul was personal or technical.

## Stalling

It is the responsibility of the team in possession of the ball to move it into the goal area. The team has 10 seconds from the time it brings the ball over the midline to get it into the offensive zone. A team in possession of the ball in the offensive zone cannot be penalized for stalling unless it has been warned by the official to keep it in. The stall warning remains in effect until a goal is scored, the defensive team gains possession of the ball, or a period ends, resulting in a face-off. After a team has been warned, stalling is called if the ball leaves the goal area in any way other than a shot on goal or by being touched by the defensive team. During the last 2 minutes of regulation play, stalling rules are in effect for the team that is ahead. In tied games, neither team is forced to keep it in the offensive zone unless warned to keep it in. At the collegiate level, the stalling rule may be initiated at any time the officials feel that the team in possession of the ball is not making an attempt to attack the opponent's goal. If officials feel that the offensive team is guilty of stalling, they will give a hand signal. This notifies the team that the stalling rule is in effect. At this time the official starts a 20-second clock that he carries with him. After the 20 seconds has expired, he gives a visual 10-second hand count. The offensive team loses possession unless it has taken a shot that hits the pipe and they regain possession. In this situation, a new 30-second clock commences. In any other situation, the 10-second hand count continues to run. When it expires, the team loses possession.

## Illegal Procedure

Any action by players that does not conform to the game rules and regulations is considered to be an illegal procedure. The following are examples:

- Touching the ball
- Putting the stick in the face of an opponent
- Team arriving late (if it was avoidable) or delaying the game
- Entering the game from the penalty area before authorized to do so by the timekeeper
- A player out of bounds participating in the play of the game
- Leaving the restraining area before the whistle is blown to start play at the time of a face-off
- Failing to remain 5 yards from the player having a free play
- Violating of the rules for substituting players, rules relating to the goal crease area (repeated violations are penalized as unsportsmanlike conduct), rules for time-outs, or rules on position for a face-off
- Having more than 10 players in the game at any time, including a player or players in the penalty area

- The head coach making two or more requests in which no violations are found for either counting long crosses or inspecting an opponent's equipment
- Having more than four long crosses in the game
- Failure by the player in possession of the ball to place it directly on the field or hand it to the nearest official on a change of possession
- Failing to advance the ball beyond the center line into the goal area in 10 seconds
- Failing to provide an acceptable horn. The horn alerts the officials to recognize activity at the scorer's table.
- Failing to have a properly equipped designated goalie on the field of play

## Conduct Foul

A coach is not allowed to enter the field of play while the game is in progress without the permission of an official. During play, the coach is restricted to the coach's area.

## Warding Off

A player in possession of the ball cannot use his free hand or arm or any other part of his body to hold, push, or control the direction of the movement of the stick or body of the player applying the check. He may protect his stick with his hand or arm or other part of his body when his opponent makes an attempt to check his stick.

## Withholding Ball From Play

When a loose ball is on the ground, a player may not lay on the ball or trap it with his stick in an attempt to withhold the ball from play. A player, players, or team cannot deliberately withhold the ball from play. Repeated actions of this nature will be ruled as unsportsmanlike conduct.

For a more complete explanation of high school rules, see *Boys Lacrosse Rule Book*, published by the National Federation of State High School Associations, P.O. Box 690, Indianapolis, IN 46206.

For a more complete explanation of the collegiate rules, see *Lacrosse Rules and Interpretations*, published by the National Collegiate Athletic Association (NCAA), P.O. Box 6222, Indianapolis, IN 46206-6222.

# CHAPTER 2

# Fundamental Skills and Drills

Mastering fundamental lacrosse skills is vital to keeping your team in the game. All are skills a team can control and none requires special athletic skills. This chapter covers stick handling and ground balls.

## HOLDING THE STICK

The first thing a beginner must learn is how to hold the stick. Right-handed players should hold the stick with the left hand on the butt of the stick and the right hand on the shaft of the stick about the distance of the length from the elbow to the fingertips (see figure 2.1). The left hand on the butt uses a full grasp. The thumb on the right hand stays on the side of the stick, guiding the shaft. From proper stick holding, we can proceed to ball-handling techniques.

## CRADLING THE BALL

After learning how to hold the stick, the player must learn how to cradle the ball. The object of the cradle is to keep the ball out of the throat of the stick and in the pocket. The easiest way to teach this to a beginner is to demonstrate it. At first you can teach a beginner to get the feel of the cradle by putting the stick in a horizontal position. Then demonstrate the cradle in a vertical position showing how the upper hand controls most of the action. Many beginners have a tendency to overcradle. You only need enough cradle to keep the ball in the pocket of the stick.

Teach beginners to cradle from a stationary position. Once they get the feel and are able to maintain ball control while cradling, let them jog. Once they can jog and maintain control of the ball, they should try running. Every

**Figure 2.1** Proper stick grip for a right-handed player.

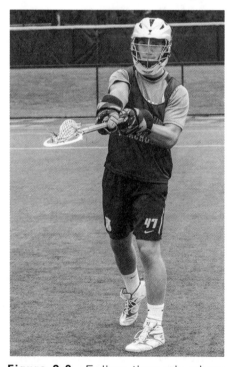

**Figure 2.2** Follow-through when passing the ball.

time they jog to the field or around the field as part of their warm-up before practice, have them cradle, switch hands, and roll-dodge while jogging. A roll dodge is discussed in chapter 3. The best way to master the cradling technique is through repetition.

## THROWING THE BALL

Like cradling, the best way to introduce of the mechanics of throwing is by demonstration. Have the players stand sideways. Right-handed players put the left foot forward. Hold the stick up at about a 60-degree vertical position. To throw the ball, they should step with their left foot and throw the ball with their upper hand. This action is similar to throwing a baseball, but with a lacrosse stick. They throw and aim with the upper hand and pull and follow through with the bottom hand (see figure 2.2). For beginners, emphasize that the lower hand ends up at the elbow of the other arm on the follow-through. We call this cracking the elbow. This ensures that the passes are made overhand. To throw, slightly cradle the ball and then step and follow through during the throwing motion. If the ball comes out low, the player is probably not cradling the ball to get it out of the pocket. When learning the mechanics of throwing, players should start from a stationary position under the supervision of the coach. Once they have mastered the fundamentals of throwing from a stationary position, they can throw from a jog and then while running during drills. Like all skills, this is best learned through repetition. This skill can be learned through individual practice at the wall. For a list of wall drills, see chapter 12, Special Situations.

## CATCHING THE BALL

Catching the ball is somewhat similar to catching a baseball. You reach out with your stick and eye (watch) the ball into your stick. As the ball enters your stick, you give back slightly to receive the ball as you would do with a baseball and glove. In lacrosse, we call this a soft stick so that the ball doesn't bounce out (see figure 2.3). In baseball you do it for the same reason but also to reduce the sting of the catch. It's important that you catch the ball in front of your body so that you can better eye it into your stick. If your stick is out to the side, it is difficult to catch the ball.

When beginners catch and throw in pairs, players should be 10 to 15 yards apart, and each pair should have its own ball. Coaches should diligently observe and correct fundamental errors in catching, throwing, and stick handling. It is important that beginners learn the correct technique from the start.

**Figure 2.3** Using a soft stick to catch the ball.

## SCOOPING GROUND BALLS

The skill of scooping is simple, but it must be performed correctly every day to master it. The amount of time spent in practice depends on the level and ability of the players. The younger and less experienced they are, the more time they should spend perfecting scooping. Even high-level teams should drill it every day for a short period.

Scooping is by far the most important skill beginners must learn. The more inexperienced the player and the team, the more the ball will be on the ground. Before a player is able to catch and throw, he must first get possession of the ball, which will be on the ground. As the player approaches the ball, he must have two hands on the stick (see figure 2.4a). The stick should be held to the side of the body with the upper hand held loosely near the throat of the stick. As he approaches the ball, he should bend with the knees and the back. He should focus on the ball, stay low, keep his head over the ball, and place the stick on the ground 6 to 10 inches in front of the ball. As he scoops the ball into the stick, the player should come up, cradle slightly (see figure 2.4b), sprint for 10 yards (see figure 2.4c), and circle as he keeps his body between his man and his stick (see figure 2.5).

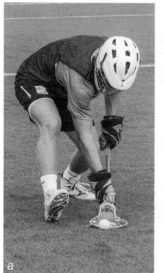

**Figure 2.4** Ground ball scoop: *(a)* approach the ball, *(b)* scoop, and *(c)* explode.

**Figure 2.5** Circling to the outside.

# GROUND-BALL DRILLS

The following are four ground-ball drills to work on every day. At the beginning of the season you might spend 1 minute on each, ensuring that each drill is performed at 100 percent speed and 100 percent efficiency. Coaches should supervise and enforce compliance of effort and technique. If the group is running a drill properly, each group of eight or nine members should get at least two or maybe three repetitions within a minute or less. Organize each drill so that every pass is backed up. Make extra balls available so they can be put into play if a ball is missed. The ball must move constantly in every drill so there is no downtime if someone misses the ball. The key is executing these fundamentals at 100 percent speed with constant movement so the players can complete as many reps as possible in the allotted amount of time. Repetition is the key.

## GROUND BALLS AWAY DRILL

### Purpose

This drill works on one of the most important skills in the game: To develop proper technique for gaining possession of a ball that is moving away from you. The turn helps you escape the pressure that is sure to come from others who are attempting to gain control of the ball.

### Setup

A player or coach stands on the side and rolls the ball away from the first player in the ground-ball line.

### Execution

The player approaches the ball with two hands on the stick, scoops it into his stick and protects his stick (see figure 2.6).

### Coaching Points

Your bottom hand at the end of the stick should be as close to the ground as possible. Your head should be low and over the ball as close as possible. Run hard as you scoop the ball. When you gain control, explode for 10 yards and turn to the outside.

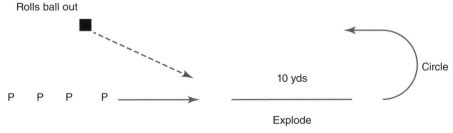

**Figure 2.6**   Ground balls away drill.

# KICK-OUT DRILL

## Purpose

To learn to kick out a ball at your feet and then scoop it if you're being challenged or to drop-step then scoop the ball if you are unchallenged.

## Setup

A player or coach drops the ball in front of the first player in the scooping drill.

## Execution

This stationary-ball drill uses nearly the same technique as the ground balls away drill, with a few variations. Kick the ball out and then scoop it, applying the same fundamentals as in the ground-ball away drill: Scoop, explode, circle, and protect your stick (see figure 2.7).

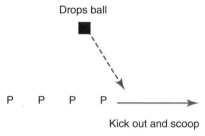

**Figure 2.7**   Kick-out drill.

## Coaching Points

This drill reinforces proper body positioning and moving quickly to the ball from a stationary position. Emphasize that the players should kick out, box out, and scoop.

## BOX-OUT DRILL

### Purpose

Box out your opponent in an attempt to gain possession.

### Setup

The coach throws the ball out. The first man in the line is the primary scooper, and the second man tries to prevent him from getting the ball.

### Execution

The first man should box out, get position on the ball, and then scoop it while using his body to prevent the defender from checking his stick (see figure 2.8).

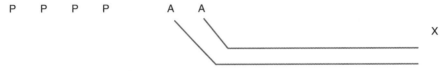

**Figure 2.8**  Box-out drill.

### Coaching Points

The player should box out as he runs to get in position to scoop the ball. He should not stop and box out when he gets to the ball and then attempt to scoop it.

# BUTT-TO-BUTT DRILL

## Purpose

Learn to drop low and box out until you can locate the ball when it is directly below you and difficult to see or when you know it's nearby but you are being strongly challenged.

## Setup

Two players stand facing away from each other. A third player drops the ball between them out of their sight and calls go.

## Execution

On the go signal, drop your body low with a wide base and begin to box out your defender until you are able to locate the ball. This happens quite often in a game (see figure 2.9).

## Coaching Points

Introduce, demonstrate, drill, and reinforce techniques. Emphasize that the head should be over the ball, the stick should be low, and the body should be dropped low.

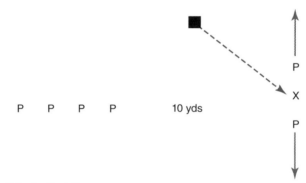

**Figure 2.9** Butt-to-butt drill.

*Team Commitment*
Every player puts 100 percent effort into every drill.

# LINE DRILLS

Proper passing and catching techniques are vital and must be practiced every day. College and some high school teams have been moving away from practicing line drills, which is probably the reason so many of the best programs in the country have players who consistently ignore the fundamentals of proper technique.

All good teams have strong fundamentals. Line drills teach and reinforce proper technique in a relatively short time. Some coaches believe that players have mastered the fundamentals by the time they get to an advanced level and no longer need to practice them. However, even if players once executed good fundamentals, if they do not practice and reinforce them every day, their skills will deteriorate. Line drills can also be used for conditioning and to teach practice tempo. If designed properly, line drills give the players many repetitions to hone their stick skills.

It is more important for players to execute successfully 50 percent of the time going at 100 percent speed, than to execute 100 percent going at only 50 percent speed. No team has won a championship at 50 percent speed, and no player has made All-American going 50 percent. The only way you can improve your efficiency at 100 percent is to practice at 100 percent. This achieves two elements for success: improved efficiency and conditioning. Players must be able to perform when they are tired. If you perform the drills properly at 100 percent speed, you will not only be able to execute when you are tired, but you also will develop eye–hand coordination and conditioning at the same time.

Once the drill begins, the players continue executing it, running from line to line, even if they miss the ball. The second man in line is responsible for backing up each pass and catching a missed or deflected pass so that the drill keeps going. A player who misses a ball does not stop to retrieve the errant pass, but instead continues to run at full speed to the end of the line.

If the second player in line does not back up the errant pass, the last man in line retrieves the ball, and a coach immediately throws another ball into the drill so that the movement is constant and the drill continues. You want to maximize movement and repetition for each drill. Each drill should last no more than 1 minute. If there are eight members in the group, each player should get at least four repetitions per drill.

You should have 7 to 12 players per group; 8 or 9 is ideal. Groups should be arranged 30 to 40 yards apart so they have space to run full speed. It is essential that players be able to catch and throw at full speed.

## BALL IN THE AIR: INSIDE RIGHT-HANDED DRILL

### Purpose

This drill emphasizes proper technique for the shoulder and follow-through when passing and catching by imagining a target above the receiver's shoulder. Start with this drill because it sets the tempo you want to follow throughout practice.

### Setup

In this drill, players imagine a box just above the receiver's shoulder on the stick side. The receiver keeps his stick in this box, which gives the passer a target (see figure 2.10). The passer must aim for this target every time.

### Execution

This drill should move quickly because the ball is being passed in a straight line. If the receiver misses the ball, the second man in line should back up the ball on the fly, and the drill continues. The receiver runs into

**Figure 2.10**  Keeping the stick in the box.

the ball with the stick up, providing a target for the passer. The receiver takes one quick cradle and then immediately releases the pass (see figure 2.11). If the group consists of 8 to 10 players, each player should get at least four repetitions in a minute.

### Coaching Points

Emphasize stick position when receiving and catching the ball directly over the shoulder.

**Figure 2.11**  Ball in the air: inside right-handed drill.

## Variation: Outside Right-Handed

Run this drill the same as the inside right-handed drill, but players make passes across their bodies to the outside of the oncoming player. It is a little more difficult to back up the feeds in this drill because the second player in line may not be able to catch the ball because the angle may be too far away from him. In this case, the last man in line retrieves the ball, and a coach throws another ball into the drill. The fundamentals emphasized are the same as in the previous drill (see figure 2.12).

**Figure 2.12**   Outside right-handed drill.

## Variation: Inside or Outside Left-Handed

This drill is the same as the first drill except players throw and receive left-handed. The fundamentals are the same, but backing up may become more of a priority if this is the weak hand for most players.

### Variation: Over-the-Shoulder Right-Handed

The purpose of this drill is to feed players cutting away up the field. The passers and receivers must move in this drill. The feeder passes over the shoulder of the receiver, who is breaking up field and is in line with the passer who is waiting to feed the line breaking out on the other side of the field. Keep the drill going in an even flow to maximize the time receiving and passing the ball and limit the time retrieving errant passes. If there are errant passes, the last man in line backs up those passes and retrieves them if he misses them. In this drill, one line passes the ball right-handed and the receiver catches the ball over his shoulder right-handed. The other line, breaking the opposite way, passes left-handed to a player breaking out, looking over his shoulder to make a left-handed catch. This is the last of the line drills (see figure 2.13).

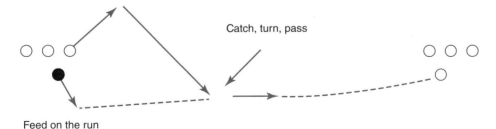

**Figure 2.13**   Over-the-shoulder right-handed drill.

# FULL-FIELD DRILLS

Full-field drills are a culminating activity after successfully teaching the fundamentals. Using the full field creates awareness of the spacing and location of teammates receiving the ball.

The following are two full-field stick-handling drills. The weave drill stresses longer upfield passes and the other stresses open-field redirects, which are part of the swarm package that will be further explained in chapter 3.

## WEAVE DRILL

### Purpose

Learn the fundamentals of passing upfield, allowing the receiver time and space to catch the ball.

### Setup

The players line up at the back line of the field and use the full length of the field. This drill is done in groups of three.

### Execution

The players on the outside pass and catch the ball right-handed on one side and left-handed on the other side. The player in the middle, if he is receiving the ball from his right, catches it right-handed and passes it right-handed. If he is receiving it from his left, he catches it left-handed and passes left-handed, thereby keeping his stick up field (see figure 2.14). Each player follows his pass.

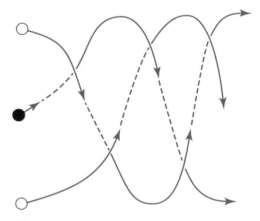

**Figure 2.14**   Weave drill.

### Coaching Points

As in all stick drills, emphasis is not on carrying the ball, but on passing it to maximize the number of passes up field. Receivers should always catch the ball upfield.

# HERE'S YOUR HELP DRILL

## Purpose

Redirect the ball to a teammate rather than to scoop and pass it. There are many times when you might not be able to gain possession of a ground ball because you are surrounded by opposing players. But you might be able to redirect the ball to a teammate who has a better chance of gaining possession. This is an important part of an offensive swarm pattern, which will be described more fully in chapter 3.

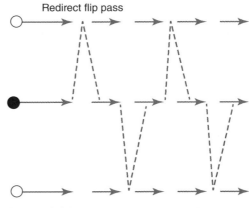

Redirect flip pass

## Setup

The drill starts with someone rolling a ball to the man in the middle, who then redirects the ball to either of the outside lanes. Instead of weaving, the players stay in their lines as they run downfield (see figure 2.15). This drill is done in groups of three.

**Figure 2.15** Here's your help drill.

## Execution

Players line up opposite each other and move to the open area, calling for the ball. Proper execution requires the player to call out loudly, "Here's your help!" and for the player over the ball to redirect the ball to the first player.

## Coaching Points

This important skill requires talking, timing, and teamwork and is an important part of the team swarm. Teams should work on it every practice.

This chapter deals with the most important skills in lacrosse, yet some teams no longer include them in their daily practice plans. No other drills can reinforce all the fundamentals of the game in such a short amount of time. These drills make up the most important 10 minutes of practice. Coaches should supervise each drill to reinforce the correct technique for each drill.

# CHAPTER 3

# Offensive Skills and Drills

Offensive skills include feeding, cutting, dodging, and shooting. This chapter explores the individual offensive skills that build the foundation for any team offense. Individual offensive skills are best demonstrated when applied to a particular offensive scheme. This chapter examines drills that apply to a specific offense: 2-2-2 deuces offense. The deuces offense uses all of the individual offensive skills. This chapter is dedicated to the drills that develop the offensive skills for individual as well as team offense.

## FEEDING FUNDAMENTALS

Feeding is to pass to an offensive player who is moving without the ball toward the goal. Feeds can be made from any location in the offensive area of the field. These locations may vary and are not limited to a specific area of the field. As we have discussed, the farther the ball travels in flight, the longer the defensive players have to recover and defend the play. For this reason, short passes are happy passes.

Feeds can be exchanged between any two players, regardless of position. Attackmen and midfielders play as a cohesive unit to create scoring opportunities.

Feeds are generally made from behind the cage, from the wing, or from up top. Proper spacing on the field is important in the feeding game. The feeder must be in a position where he can get his hands free while being covered by a defensive player. The concept of constant movement is reinforced in the feeding game. The defense attempts to block, intercept, or interrupt the timing of the feed. The feeder must create space between himself and the defender before attempting to feed. The ability of players to find space is essential to successful offense. The feeder and offensive player cutting or moving toward the goal are working together to maximize the scoring opportunity. Drills that use a progression, increasing the number of players on offense and defense, are the most effective method for introducing and reinforcing these skills. Movement by the feeder also forces the goalie to move and follow the path of the player and the ball. This creates a greater chance that the shooter will have more open goal to shoot at upon receiving the ball. Feeding and shooting drills should be directly related to your team's offensive scheme.

The teaching principles of the passing game are also valid in the feeding game. A feed is a pass to a player moving toward the goal to create a shot opportunity. Teams can also emphasize the hockey assist, which is the pass to the player who makes the pass that leads directly to a goal. Although lacrosse does not officially record a second assist, it is an important part of a successful offense and is recognized as a measure of success.

The following are basic feeding-game teaching points:

- All passes should be short, sharp, stick side, in the box, and away from the defender's stick.
- Ninety-nine percent of all passes should be overhand and made precisely when the cutter is open.
- The feeder must continue moving and faking passes so he will be able to get his stick open to feed as the cutter breaks open.
- Players keep their heads up at all times to see cutting offensive players.
- Passes should be made to players who are moving; players should not reward a teammate who is standing flat footed. This creates a greater chance for a turnover.
- Players create space between themselves and defenders through constant movement. This forces the defender to focus his energy on running with the player, not throwing checks.
- Passes should be precise and to the target to allow the receiver to catch, cradle, and shoot the ball.
- Players should value the ball and not force the action. If the player is not open, keep working for the next opportunity.
- Players should protect the stick by keeping it between their body and the defender.
- Players should use body and stick fakes to prevent the feed from being blocked.
- Players should anticipate a teammate moving to the open area.
- A feed should be timed to minimize the ability of the defender to check the stick of the cutting offensive player.
- Passes are made to the stick side and slightly lead the cutter so the ball arrives on the stick as he prepares to shoot.

# CUTTING FUNDAMENTALS

Cutting is an integral part of a successful offense. Constant movement by attackmen and midfielders creates a pattern and flow that occupy the defensive players. The use of timely cuts and accurate feeding techniques puts pressure on the defense and goalie to increase scoring chances. Defensive players working against active cutting offensive players are also unable to be part of the team defense slide package. These are used to prevent the offense from taking advantage of 1v1 dodging situations.

The majority of the cutting game also results in the offensive player moving toward the goal where a higher-percentage shot can be taken. It is important for the offensive players to remain in a balanced set when using the cutting game. Random cuts create gridlock in the offensive area of the field.

Coaches should teach the following concepts: Move without the ball, pass and cut, and go without the ball. These concepts keep the defense occupied while the offense attempts to create a scoring opportunity by breaking down the defense.

Proper stick protection by the cutter is required to successfully receive the feed and deliver the shot. The ability to screen the defender with the body while receiving the pass provides the necessary time to catch, cradle, and shoot.

The majority of cuts do not result in receiving a pass and a potential scoring opportunity. The offensive player must continue his movement to reset the offense and balance the field. The following points allow a greater opportunity to score:

- You must continue moving at all times.
- Protect your stick by keeping your body between your stick and your defender.
- Get open either by using picks or beating your man using a backdoor cut.
- Time your cuts; quality counts above quantity.
- Do not cut if the feeder is not in a favorable position to make a pass or cutters are already in the area.
- If a high-percentage shot is not available after receiving the ball on a cut, carry the ball out and make the next pass.
- Balance the field with proper spacing and movement. All offensive players should be in synch with each other.
- Do not create a transition or fast-break opportunity for the defensive team. Keep a minimum of one offensive player at the top of the box area.
- Use fakes to gain a step on the defensive player. Changing hands (right to left; left to right), speed, and direction are recommended.
- Remember there are 13 players in the offensive area. Each cut creates movement of at least two players (offense and defense). It is difficult for a cutting game to run through crowded areas successfully.

- Cutters should be prepared to have their stick checked while the ball is in flight or immediately upon receiving the feed. Use your body and proper stick protection techniques.
- Two-man plays, bow tie, and the pick-and-roll, are effective for creating scoring opportunities in a cutting game. Timing and proper spacing are keys of successful team offense.
- Put the shot on cage and force the goalie to make the save.

# SWARMING

Swarming refers to a team concept in which all six offensive players react to all loose balls in their offensive half of the field. The two players closest to the ball must react as quickly as possible and go directly to it to get possession. The other four players all have lanes and spots they must fill as quickly as possible. Teams want two players on the ball, three players in an umbrella 10 yards from the ball upfield, and one player 10 yards from the ball directly downfield. Three players upfield prevent the opposing team from gaining possession of the ball and initiating a transition. The offense has an advantage on loose balls because all defenses are taught to play between the goal and the offensive player they are covering. The offense will have at least one extra man to participate in the swarm, putting them in better position to either come up with possession or check the defensive players who might have position on the ball. That extra man is usually the offensive creaseman because not only is he usually close to the ball, but also his defensive player is responsible for the defensive hole. The defensive hole is the defensive area directly in front of the crease. The aim is not only to outnumber but also to outhustle the defensive players (see figure 3.1).

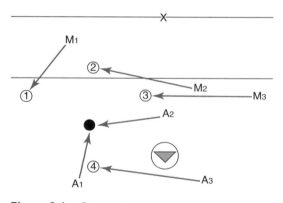

**Figure 3.1** Swarming.

Figure 3.1 shows three midfielders in the umbrella and two attackmen closest to the ball. In situations in which one midfielder or more is closest to the ball, the attackmen have to fill in those positions in the umbrella. For example, if M2 and A1 are closest to the ball, M3 fills the number 2 spot in the umbrella, and A3 fills the number 3 spot. The offensive formation and the location of the loose ball determine which players are closest to the ball and who must fill the three positions in the umbrella. The closest man to the sideline is always responsible for the number 1 spot. The next closest man is responsible for the number 2 spot, and the man farthest from the ball occupies the number 3 spot. All three men in the umbrella are approximately 10 yards above the ball. They call "help" to their team- mates who are fighting for the ball to let them know they are in position so their teammates can redirect the ball to them.

When the offensive team gains possession, the team pushes the ball downfield to the nearest attackman (A1). A1 looks to the crease for an opening (A2). If there isn't one, he passes it to X (A3). A3 immediately looks to the onside crease to A2; if he is not open, A3 brings it to the offside looking for the inside lane (M2) (option 1). Option 2 is the out- side lane (M3). If not open, the two midfielders stay high for a time and room shot, where the shooter has space and can free his hands. A3 penetrates the goal line extended and forces a 3v2 with himself and the two midfielders on the weak side. The best time to attack the goal is when gaining possession after an unsettled situation (see figure 3.2).

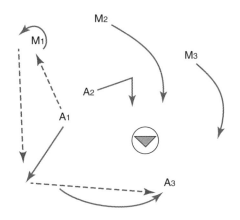

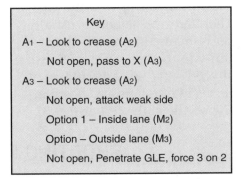

| Key |
| --- |
| A1 – Look to crease (A2) |
| Not open, pass to X (A3) |
| A3 – Look to crease (A2) |
| Not open, attack weak side |
| Option 1 – Inside lane (M2) |
| Option – Outside lane (M3) |
| Not open, Penetrate GLE, force 3 on 2 |

**Figure 3.2**   Swarm possession to slow break.

## Offensive Swarm

Offensive swarming is the most important aspect of a lacrosse game. The following statistics illustrate my point. In December of 2003, I was asked to speak at the United States Intercollegiate Lacrosse Association (USILA) national convention. I was given the opportunity to select my topic, so I chose ground balls and team swarming. In preparation for this presentation I did a 10-year analysis of our ground-ball and clearing and riding statistics. I was astounded by the results. I knew all along that we had dominated ground balls, but I never realized to what extent. I used the period from 1994 to 2003. During this period we averaged 17 more possessions per game than our opponents from ground balls. This equates to eight or nine shots a game and probably three or four goals. I retired after the 2009 season with a 17-year winning percentage of 84. I attribute this primarily to our ground-ball dominance. The most important thing about this aspect of the game is that any team can excel at it. It doesn't take skill, speed, or great stick work to master it. It only takes hard work, hustle, and perseverance by players and the coaching staff.

## Defensive Swarm

Swarming on the defensive half of the field is different from swarming on the offensive half. In fact, technically speaking, it is not a swarm of the complete defense. Only the defensive player directly in the area of a loose ball can aggressively go after the ball. The other defensive players must remain at their positions between the man they are covering and the goal. Therefore, the defense is usually outnumbered in terms of proximity to the ball, so the offense should have an advantage in terms of numbers and positioning on the ball (see figure 3.3).

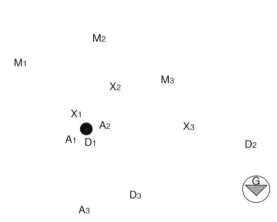

**Figure 3.3** Defensive swarm.
Key: D = defenseman; X = defensive midfielder and long-stick midfielder; A = attackman; M = offensive midfielder

# SHOOTING FUNDAMENTALS

Shooting techniques are an extension of the fundamentals of throwing and passing introduced in chapter 2. Progress in this skill set should result in the shot being on cage. The lacrosse goal is 6 feet wide by 6 feet high. Beginning players should be able to hit that area with a lacrosse ball 100 percent of the time. Earlier discussions about catching and throwing introduced the idea of throwing the ball to the box, the area above the stick-side shoulder and parallel to the head of the player receiving the ball. The box can further be described as the head of the stick that is placed in a position to catch the ball.

During the course of play, the following can occur when a shot is taken in an attempt to score:

- The shot is blocked or deflected by a player or stick and does not reach the goal area.
- The goalie blocks the ball with his stick or body but is unable to control the ball, creating a rebound or second shot opportunity (similar to an offensive rebound in basketball).
- The goalie makes the save by securing the ball in his stick and looks to start the clearing game.

- The shot misses the cage and is loose on the ground in the defensive end of the field.
- The shot misses the cage or hits the pipe and goes out of bounds (the player closest to the exit location of the ball is awarded possession).
- The shot goes past the goalie and scores for the offensive team.

Coaches emphasize shooting accuracy simply because shots on goal that score are the only results that favor the offense. The other result, a goalie save, provides an opportunity for the offense to use the riding game in an attempt to get the ball back. The percentage of goals scored, shots on goal, and total shots attempted are important statistical categories to be evaluated.

Shooting techniques are an extension of passing fundamentals. As we noted earlier, the same principles are in effect; however, you are passing to a 6-by-6-foot defined goal area. Shoot at a higher rate of speed when attempting to score.

- Place the stick directly above your head with both hands and gradually lower it at full extension along the side of your body until the stick is directly underhand at your feet. This simulates the range of shooting speed vs. accuracy in our sport. The overhand shot is more accurate, but slower; the underhand shot is less accurate, but faster. The sidearm shot is the halfway point, with equal amounts of speed and accuracy.
- Depending on your skill level, categorize high-percentage shots based on the distance from the cage.
- Bounce shots should always hit on or inside the goal area crease line to prevent the ball bouncing over the cage.
- Always shoot before practice or games during a preparation period. Grass fields and field turf vary greatly depending on weather conditions, which affects bounce shots.
- When shooting, change the plane of your stick. This forces the goalie to move and anticipate the shot location. Shooting high to low or low to high increases shooting percentage. Rapid ball movement forces the goalie to move and allows you more open area in your attempt to score.
- Remembering to shoot to net further reinforces of the importance of shooting the ball into the 6-by-6-foot goal area. High or wide shots have no chance of becoming goals.
- The head of the stick should always follow through along the path of the ball. This ensures the ball is on target.
- Proper lower-body positioning creates upper-body positioning. The movement of the front hip and stepping through the shot on the follow-through motion is essential.
- The three-quarter shot is considered most effective because it strikes the proper balance between speed and accuracy. Your top hand is over your

shoulder and follows through according to the throwing techniques. As the top hand follows through, the bottom hand pulls down, creating torque on the body and stick.

- The sidearm shot is effective in a step-down situation, when dropping the head of the stick halfway can still provide an accurate shot on the cage. Remember, what you gain in speed, you lose in accuracy.

- Use the one-hand shot close to the cage when you are unable to get both hands free. It is taken mostly when dodging to the goal from 3 to 5 yards.

- Take the underhand shot with the head of the stick at or below the knees. Remember, even more than the sidearm shot, what you gain in speed, you lose in accuracy. It is difficult for the head of the stick to follow through the path of the ball and get the shot on cage.

- The backhand shot is effective when you have run out your angle and must rely on the backward action to get the ball on cage. It is also used where both the offensive and defensive players are screening the goalie and the element of surprise creates a scoring opportunity.

# DODGING FUNDAMENTALS

Every offensive player must be able to use the threat of a dodge as an offensive weapon. You don't have to be a great dodger to be a good offensive player. But you have to be able to threaten to dodge so that you can create space to feed.

Dodging should be practiced every day so that you are able to recognize when the defensive player has made an error either by position or by overcommitment. Some players are quick enough to initiate dodges. Others must be able to take advantage of defensive errors. It is all part of the offensive philosophy. You must be able to take what the defense gives you.

## Power Sweep

The power sweep is a simple acceleration or runaround dodge. This is the first dodge you should master. You can execute it even if the defender is quicker than you are. Run hard at your man and when you get close to him, simply plant your outside foot and cut hard to the open space toward the goal. You will be able to get a step on your man because you know where he is going. The only way the defender can stop you is by stepping into you and attempting to stop you by applying a hold. The countermove to this is the roll dodge.

## Roll Dodge

This dodge can only be used when the defensive player attempts to use a hold or his body to turn back the power sweep. When contact is made, the offensive player simply plants his inside foot and rolls back in the opposite direction. The first step off of the roll must be toward the cage. The body of the dodger must be in contact with and roll off of the defender. The offensive player uses the momentum of the defender to roll inside toward the cage.

## Split Dodge

This dodge is sometimes called the face dodge and is probably the most effective because it is the quickest and most dangerous. The player executing this dodge poses an immediate threat to pass or shoot because he has already penetrated the defense.

These three dodges require proper footwork. Practice them every day. Early in the year, practice them without opposition. This gives the players an opportunity to concentrate on speed, footwork, and execution. When they first go one-on-one, the defender should go at half-speed so that both he and offensive player can focus on footwork. The defender plays token defense, but the offensive player should work on footwork and stick protection at full speed. The offensive player must be able to perfect the fundamentals of each dodge and know when to use each one. He can initiate a dodge, but it will only be effective if the defensive player violates a defensive fundamental. The dodger has to be able to read this and react accordingly.

# OFFENSIVE DRILLS

Using drills for the sake of drilling is not recommended. Each drill should teach a specific skill, help the skill become second nature to the players, and play a vital part of your offense. The stick-work drills you use in practice should be geared to your team's offensive pattern. The following drills can be used in many types of offenses. The first set of drills outlined is geared for the deuces offense, which incorporates many of the individual offensive skills, such as dodging, feeding, cutting, and setting picks. Deuces uses a 2-2-2 offensive pattern, with two players behind the cage (these are usually attackmen), two on the crease (usually one attackman and one midfielder), and two up top (usually midfielders). However, you can use any combination depending on your players. The deuces offense is a series of two-man games incorporated within a six-man coordinated offense. The deuces offense uses the bow-tie and seal-overload maneuvers.

# FEEDING BOW-TIE DRILL

## Purpose

Teach the basic pick-and-cut on the crease and a second cut by the pick man to the backside. The first step in the deuces offense is the bow tie, which is a basic pick-and-cut on the crease and a second cut by the pickman to the backside.

## Setup

Two men set up on the crease, and a ball carrier or feeder is behind the goal.

## Execution

As an attackman drives onside to the goal line extended (GLE), he attempts to execute a key maneuver in the deuces offense: feeding bow tie. His inside foot hitting the GLE is the signal for the onside crease cutter (M3) to break open (option 1). (See figure 3.4.) If M3 is not open, the attackman steps back and on his second step and looks to the pickman (A2) cutting back door to the opposite pipe (option 2).

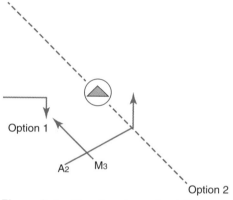

**Figure 3.4** Feeding bow tie drill.

## Coaching Points

The attackmen should be able to keep the ball behind and be confident they can control the ball and continue to put pressure on the defense. Even if the attackmen cannot beat their defender or force a slide, they will be able to get separation at the GLE because most defensemen will be playing top side at the GLE. This means that the defenseman will be in position to turn the attackmen back behind the cage at the GLE. This will enable the attackman to step back, get separation, and have a short window of time to feed.

# SEAL-OVERLOAD DRILL

## Purpose

Learn how to get open when the defenders are zoning the crease attack players.

## Setup

The play is set up similar to the bow tie, with two men on the crease and a ball carrier behind the goal.

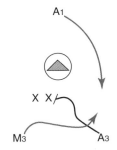

## Execution

The midfielder (M3) breaks off the pick by the attackman (A2) and cuts onside pipe when the feeder (A1) plants his inside foot at the GLE. If M3 executes his drive properly and drives his man into the pick, he should be open (see figure 3.5).

**Figure 3.5** Seal overload drill.

## Coaching Points

- If the defense reads the pick and switches, then M3 seals his defenseman on his side (M3 sets a pick and seals his defenseman toward the crease). The pickman (A2), instead of cutting toward the offside pipe, reverses his cut and pops out high toward the onside of M3. A2 is now in an overload on the ball side.

- A1 can drive once, but no more than twice to the GLE. If A1 does not find an open man on the crease, he should give the ball up to the other attackman behind the goal.

# FEEDING DRILL FOR DEUCES

## Purpose

The following drill works on timing and distance for the bow-tie feeds and crease bow-tie cuts. The stick-work drill shown in figure 3.6 is a timing and spacing drill without opposition. It follows the basic setup for stick drills. Players are in lines, sticks in the box, feet moving, and using rapid progression.

## Execution

Concentrate on the timing for the onside cut (option 1), and then add the offside cut (option 2). See figure 3.6.

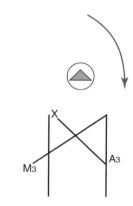

**Figure 3.6** Feeding drill for deuces.

## Coaching Points

If neither man is fed, they immediately reset approximately 8 yards above the GLE. Because this drill establishes the timing of both the bow-tie feeds and the bow-tie crease cuts, A1 drives to the GLE three times to force the creasemen (A3 and M3) to pick and reset for timing and spacing.

## DRILLS FOR TIMING THE BOW TIE

The following drills, shown in figures 3.7 to 3.9, are competitive drills with active defenders. Each drill follows the same setup and execution. All these drills isolate important parts of the offense. Once players master the individual parts, put them together for the complete offensive package.

### Setup

Begin as in a 3v2 drill and work your way up to a 4v4 drill. In the 3v2 drill, the feeder is uncovered, which gives him an opportunity to learn how to read the defense.

### Execution

The feeder, working on his timing and footwork, has the opportunity to read the defense without being concerned that a defender is guarding him. After the two creasemen (A2 and M3) learn the timing and spacing, add a third defenseman to cover the attack man at X (3v3).

### BOW TIES (3V2)

In the 3v2, defenders cover the two crease-men, and the feeder at X is uncovered.

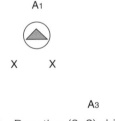

**Figure 3.7**   Bow ties (3v2) drill.

An attackman (A1) works on feeding the bow tie. The onside creaseman (A2) picks for the offside creaseman (M3) at the offside pipe about 5 yards off the GLE (see figure 3.7). The drill emphasizes that the onside cut (M3) drives off the pick by A2 as the feeder (A1) plants his foot at the GLE. The pass to the onside cutter is made on the first step back from the GLE. The feed to the offside cutter (A2) is made on the second step back from the GLE.

### BOW TIES (3V3)

This drill is the same as the 3v2, but adds a third defenseman (see figure 3.8). The feeding attackman must drive hard from X to the cage as if he were going to shoot. He must believe he is a threat to dodge and shoot at all times. If he beats his man, he must read the defense and react accordingly. If no defensive player slides to back up and cover him and he has beaten his man, he must be able to shoot. If someone slides to him, he must read the defense and find the open man. The key is to teach all offensive players how to read the defense and find the open men. This can only be accomplished through practice and repetition. A portion of practice has to be devoted to this teaching technique every day.

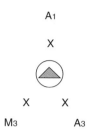

A1

X

X     X
M3          A3

**Figure 3.8**   Bow ties (3v3) drill.

The second part of the drill is for the attackman to get separation from his defenseman, which allows space to feed. This is the most important part of the bow tie because you can't always count on beating the defenseman, but you can always create separation so that you have space to feed. It is important for players to master these skills. Although there are many aspects of the game that you may not be able to control, you can control this aspect of the game. Feeding bow tie and shooting bow tie demand nearly perfect execution to be effective. They must be practiced every day.

## BOW TIES (4V4)

Add a second feeder to work on mirroring, roll throwbacks, and timing maneuvers. Mirroring is when two players, usually one with the ball and the other without the ball, rotate to position themselves directly across from one another. Typically, this involves rotating around the crease. The two attackmen behind can work on their two-man game as well as their bow-tie feeds. They can either mirror each other or pick for each other behind (see figure 3.9). The attackmen only feed when the timing is right. They control the offense. It is comparable to a football quarterback. In lacrosse, whoever has the ball controls the tempo. If players are patient and execute, they will control the game. This is the area they are able to control.

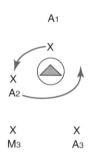

A1

X

X
A2

X        X
M3        A3

**Figure 3.9**   Bow ties (4v4) drill.

# MIDFIELDER DRILLS

Although deuces is an attack-oriented offense, the midfielders are still an important part of the offense. When the ball is behind the goal, the first responsibility of the midfielders is to keep the field balanced so they can back up feeds to the crease. They must also read their defenseman and cut to an open area if their man has dropped off to a backup position. If this occurs, they must cut to the open area and receive a pass, which leads to a shot. The offside midfielder's open lane is usually down the backside, or what is referred to as the skip lane (an adjacent passing lane). The onside midfielder has three options. If his defender has dropped in to back up, he can cut back door to the crease, he can pop out to provide an outlet option, or, if he has the ball, he can pass or carry the ball up top. When the midfielder has the ball on top, a series of two-man options, called the 20 series, is available. These are four basic plays that can work together.

## 21 CLEAR OUT

The off-ball midfielder clears through then pops out for the ball carrier.

## 22 PICK-OFF MAN PICKS FOR THE BALL CARRIER

This comes off an isolation pass or give-and-go.

## 23 WEAVE AND FLIP

The ball carrier flips the ball off a weave to his teammate and cuts inside for a possible return pass. A flip is when the inside player on the weave pops the ball up in the air so that the outside player can catch it in full stride. The inside player must use his body to protect his stick from his defender in this maneuver. The player receiving the flip catches the ball with his stick to the outside and his body between his man and his stick.

## 24 FAKE FLIP

The ball carrier fakes to his teammate and either dodges to the cage or looks to pass to another midfielder who has cut to the cage.

# 2V2 PICK DRILLS

Pick drills are the most basic offensive drills in the game. All offenses benefit from the skills learned in these drills. The Canadian-style game begins and ends with these drills. Timing, spacing, and reading your defensive opponent are essential. The in-tight, stick-handling skills necessary to execute pick drills effectively can only be taught by working the drills live. These skills can only be learned by repetition in gamelike conditions. The following drills can be used either with or without competition.

## PICK-AND-SLIP DRILL

The ball carrier must read the opponent's defenseman to see whether he is in position to double the ball. If the defender playing the man who is setting the pick steps up to pick up the ball carrier on a switch, the pickman cuts behind the man who picked up the ball carrier (see figure 3.10).

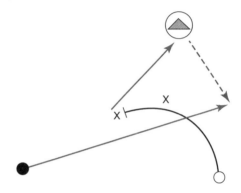

**Figure 3.10**　Pick-and-slip drill.

## PICK-AND-ROLL DRILL

If the defender playing the pickman plays too wide or cheats to pick up the ball carrier, the pickman simply rolls inside (front side) before the ball carrier gets to the pick (see figure 3.11).

These options are executed only when the defender playing the pickman is positioned high to double the ball. He can only double the ball effectively if he positions himself up near the pickman. Once he does this, both offensive players must read his defensive vulnerability and react accordingly. Every time a defense is aggressive, the offense must read this and take advantage of opportunities to penetrate the defense.

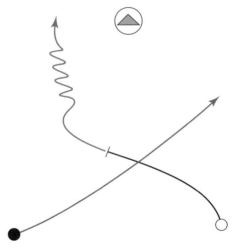

**Figure 3.11**　Pick-and-roll drill.

If the defenders are playing it straight and not attempting to double the ball off of a pick, then the offensive players still have several options. The first purpose of setting up a pick is for the ball carrier to time his drive so he can run his man into the pickman. To help accomplish this, the ball carrier must execute his drive to the cage at full speed to force his man to play him, and him alone, with full concentration while trying to keep up with him. If the ball carrier catches his man turning his head in the direction of the pick, he should split-dodge and immediately penetrate the defense in the opposite direction. If his man plays it properly and they both run hard, it is essential that the ball carrier drive his defender into the pickman. The ball carrier's first option is to drive past the defender, who is switching to pick him up. This should be possible because the defender switching onto him was dropping off of the pickman in anticipation of the switch call. He had been in a relatively stationary position so that the offensive player driving off the pick has speed and momentum on his side. If the defender is able to execute the switch successfully, then the ball carrier has a second option. The teammate who sets the pick must slip to the inside as an option to place him in a shooting position. Those players involved in tight passing and shooting maneuvers must practice with and without opposition to acquire the timing and spacing to execute these drills.

# 4V4 KEEP-AWAY DRILL

## Purpose

This is one of the best all-around lacrosse drills you can work on. It teaches participants to execute both offensively and defensively. In close quarters, this drill can be adapted to the skill level of the players.

## Setup

If possible, players wear numbered, reversible practice jerseys. If they don't have numbered jerseys, then line up players and number them 1 to 12. You need a minimum of 12 players or three teams per box. If you use two boxes, you need 24 players. Divide the group into teams of four. The area of play should be a minimum of 20 yards square. To make substitution quick and easy, each team wears a specific color. For example, group 1 wears white, group 2 wears black, and group 3 wears whatever undergarment colors they have. Two groups are in the box at a time. The group not involved in the drill (team Z) stands at the corners of the drill area. Each player on team Z has a ball that he throws into play whenever there is an errant pass. This minimizes the time lost in retrieving bad passes and keeps the drill moving. It is important to maximize the number of repetitions each player gets in this drill and to maximize conditioning.

## Execution

Players must pass the ball within 4 seconds, and each group must make five passes. Each player in the group must make at least one catch and, when this is completed, that group is declared the winner. The group steps out of the drill and gets a rest. The losing group stays in on offense and team Z joins the drill on defense. The losing group begins the next round with the ball. The winners rotate out, and the losers stay in. The idea is to go for speed at all times. This is an important part of practice for conditioning, movement, and execution. Good execution is rewarded to the winning team with rest. Poor execution by the losing team is penalized by keeping players in the drill. The losing team doesn't get a rest until it either wins the drill or the drill is over. Each rotation should only take 2 minutes from start to finish.

Although the drill is short, it teaches the following fundamentals: catching and throwing on the move, stick protection, moving off the ball and getting open, and being able to get open when being cut off. The drill also practices passing and catching in tight areas under pressure, using picks when necessary to get open, and defensively being able to pressure and cut off a player.

Good players cannot be cut off from the ball. Some players allow themselves to be cut off because they don't know how to get open, they're not in shape, or they're not as determined to do so. Whatever the reason, it becomes obvious in this drill. There is no place to hide. The good players love this drill and the less able struggle with it. As the coach, you get to see what your players are made of quickly in this drill.

Work on this drill three or four times per week in the early season. By mid-season players get good at this drill and love it when an opponent attempts to press them on defense or, better yet, tries to cut them off. If you're ready, it's easy to get open, and when you do, you have already penetrated the defense. On the other hand, if you're not ready for team pressure or cutoffs, the offense will be disrupted and it will be difficult to run your offense.

This drill prepares you to test your opponent early in the game to see whether they've done their homework. Are they ready to play under pressure and can they get open if you cut off the best players? It puts a lot of pressure on them and you can identify the players who can't handle it. A byproduct of pressure is that some teams are able to handle it for a few minutes, but as the game wears on, their lack of conditioning shows and they simply can't generate any offense. Sometimes the opposing team's best players are the ones who are out of shape, so this gives your team a decisive mental and physical advantage. This possibility has to be drilled into your team every practice. Remind them of this and reward them when they achieve the day's practice goals. Every drill is a building block to a successful practice. Every practice is an important building block for the success of the team.

## Variation: 4v4 Pressure Drill

This drill is similar to the keep-away drill, except you incorporate it into a 4v4 half-field game. The offense has the ball in the box and must take four passes against adjacent shutoff pressure. Once they complete four passes, the offense may press for a score as the defense drops into a soft man to man. With each shot, goal or not, the goalie clears the ball. Once cleared, the offense becomes the defense as the defense becomes the offense. Additional teaching points include forcing long poles in the transition game and forcing attackmen to play defense. With any loose ball or loss of possession, four passes must be completed.

# Y DRILL: FORMATIONS AND OPTIONS

This drill teaches the passing options available in the deuces set. It is another variation of the 4v4 drill in that you isolate the formations of the deuces set. In the figures that follow, only the offensive personnel are shown.

## SET 1: 1-2-1

The four offensive players are two attackmen and two midfielders. One midfielder plays on the crease. The four defenders can be any combination of three long poles and one short pole, or two of each.

### Variation: Ball Out Top 1

The emphasis in this set is on the two creasemen working on their picks and overloads. The offense has a chance to focus on the crease defensemen. It gives them an opportunity to read whether the defense is playing man to man or zone. The midfielder initiates the drill with an alley dodge, which is down the outside of the formation, driving to the goal. The two creasemen rotate away from the dodge with the off creaseman setting up a high post, the onside creaseman drops down to set up a screen, and the attackman cuts to the offside skip lane at the goal line extended. In all drills, feed first and shoot second. The options for the midfielder are first to feed the high post and second to feed the skip lane.

Other options for the midfielder include a give-and-go with the onside creaseman and a diagonal cutoff of a double pick. On a give-and-go, the man who passes the ball must first use a backdoor cut on his man and then make a V-cut directly toward the feeder. When the two crease defensive men are playing tight man to man inside, the diagonal cutoff of a double pick can be effective.

### Variation: Ball at X 1

In this set, the concentration is on coordinating the feeding to the first attackman and M2 executing the bow tie on the crease. As the attackman drives to the GLE, his options are to feed the second midfielder cutting to the onside crease (option 1), cutting to the offside crease (option 2), or the offside midfielder cutting down the skip lane. The midfielder must be ready to back up feeds to the crease as well as read crease overloads. Anytime his defensive man slides down to help out on the crease or on crease overloads, he must cut down and become an option in the skip lane.

## SET 2: 2-1-1

### Variation: Ball at X 2

The emphasis is on the 2v2 game for the attackmen. They concentrate on placing the picks behind, coming off of a pick, and looking to make a feed or shot. In addition to their picks, the timing and spacing of mirroring each other is the focus of this drill.

The second midfielder coordinates his cuts and spacing with the mirror attackman cutting through the crease. The first midfielder has the same responsibilities of backing up feeds to the crease as well as cuts down the skip lane. He executes the responsibilities of the top far-side midfielder in this set. He should read the defense, and anytime his defender ball watches or helps out on the crease, he should cut down the outside lane.

## SET 3: 1-1-2

### Variation: Ball Out Top 2

In this set, the emphasis is with the 2v2 game with the top midfielders. They work on their timing and spacing for the picks and pick-and-roll. On the pick-and-roll, the pickman reads the defensive man, playing him, and cuts inside before the ball carrier gets to the pick. As mentioned earlier, the pickman must read the defensive positioning of the man guarding him. On a switch or bingo call, he should execute the slip. Switch is a defensive technique that allows players to change their matchup to prevent an offensive advantage. Bingo is a defensive double team on the offensive player with the ball.

### Variation: Clear Out

On a clear out from up top, the offside midfielder cuts inside and curls back up, clearing the side of the field for the alley dodge. The attackmen cut to the high post and the GLE skip lane. On this option, the midfielder has the green light to go to the cage if there is no backup. Options 1 and 2 are available to him if one of the men slides to back up on the dodge.

# TEACHING POINTS

The following guidelines are from the "Attackman's Bible," courtesy of The USILA Coaches Kit.

1. Make your defenseman play you and only you alone every second you are in the game. Keep moving all the time so that he must center his attention on you and will not be able to look around and be in position to help out his fellow defensemen.

2. In moving the ball around the circle, make all passes sharp, short, and to the outside away from the defensemen's stick.

3. Make feed passes hard as a general rule; this will depend on your field position and the game situation at that time.

4. When you have the ball, never stand still. Keep moving all the time. If necessary, run backward and forward but keep moving. When you are ready to make a pass, take one step back quickly and throw. Never pass to just get rid of the ball. Always have a purpose in mind. Always bear in toward the goal. Protect your stick with your body.

5. All feed passes should be away from defenseman's stick. This may require a fake pass first. Be constantly faking; both with your body and stick.

6. Always move to meet every pass, and circle away from defenseman's stick.

7. When you have the ball, be constantly faking passes. Keep your defenseman's stick moving and notice how he reacts; his reactions will be your clue to how you are going to attack.

8. When in possession of ball, make the defenseman play your stick, watch his stick—the position of it will determine the direction of your feed and the type of dodge you might try.

9. Take pains to make every pass good. We cannot win if the opponent has the ball.

10. Never make a pass to a man who is covered just to get rid of the ball; you will only be pushing the blame to your teammate.

11. If an attackman is being ridden hard and can't dodge or get away, the nearest man on each side must go to help him.

12. On all long shots, a man must be on the crease and in position to screen ball; if he is not in a screening position, don't shoot.

13. On every screen shot, the crease-man should check up on the defenseman's stick and immediately face the goalie, so that he is ready to bat in a rebound.

14. After receiving a pass, as the ball moves around the outside, look first at the man who threw you the ball to see what he is doing, then at the crease; this must be done at all times.

15. If you receive a pass after cutting and haven't got a good shot, hold on to the ball and circle back so as to set up another situation.

16. Place all shots, usually for the far corner, and shoot hard. When within five yards of the goal the shot should be for a corner or just inside the pipe.

17. After picking up a loose ball, turn and face the crease immediately. If nobody is open, move in fast until you are picked up.

18. Don't hold the ball long. Keep it moving with quick, short, accurate passes, always having an objective in mind.

19. Always be in a position to back up every pass or shot. When a cut is made and a shot is taken, the whole attack must play a part, moving to be in a position to back the pass to the cutter and his shot.

20. Never try a dodge when men are waiting in a position to back up immediately; this is suicide.

21. Never try to force in, with the ball or by a pass, if the defense is drawn in, pull them out first.

22. Never stand close enough together so that one defenseman can cover two attackmen. Stay spread so as to spread their defense.

23. When there is a loose ball on the ground, go after it in a hurry; as a general rule, play the ball first and then the opponent. You must have the ball to win.

24. Always keep our field balanced in order that you stay in better position to back up and leave more space to work in.

25. Shoot plenty, but only if you feel you have a good shot. Don't think that just because you cut and receive a pass that you must necessarily shoot.

26. Always have at least one, most times two, men behind the goal in best position to back up shots.

27. Never try to pass to a man on the point from any position other than one definitely behind the goal. Also make sure that the man you are passing to is breaking for the point. The point being the best position from which to feed.

28. Time your cuts—that is, don't cut if the man with the ball is not watching or not in position to pass; don't cut if you are not in the pattern or if two men are already cutting. Remember someone must always back up and it may be you.

29. Make full cuts—go through and out—don't cut half speed or hang around the crease after a cut. All cuts should be at top speed and preceded by a good fake.

30. Zig your cuts. Fake with your entire body.

31. After a ball has been cleared, if you have a wide open opportunity to dodge, do it, or if you are sure a man is open, pass to him, otherwise settle the ball down and let your attack get set up. Remember after the clear your midfield needs time to catch its breath. Don't force the ball immediately after a clear unless the situation warrants it.

32. Every offensive man should try at least one dodge every game. Learn several types of dodges—at least three; the more, the better.

33. When you lose the ball, ride. Close attack must ride and ride hard until the ball is past midfield. Whenever possible, try to turn defensemen to the inside. We must control the ball, if we hope to win.

34. Don't rush at a man when riding—particularly behind the goal—force him to pass—keep your stick up and make opponent make the first move. Play him as though you were now a defensemen.

35. Always remember, teamwork is the key to a good attack, but each man must have some individualism in him or he will not be an asset to the team.

36. Know this Bible and strive to put it to use.

Team offense is one of the most important and most difficult areas to teach. It is the one area that is subject to certain uncontrollable variables. A slight failure in timing on cuts or feeds or when the offense comes upon a hot goalie can wreak havoc with most offenses. Because of this, it is essential that offensive players minimize these uncontrollable factors by perfecting the factors they can control.

The attackman at X must coordinate his movement with his teammate behind. They must mirror each other most of the time. For example, A1 has the ball at X and A2 places himself at the GLE. If A1 drives onside goal line extended, A2 clears through the crease under the two creasemen, thereby opening an option as he cuts through the crease and then rotates back to X to be available for an outlet from A1.

Deuces is a timing offense based on feeds into the crease area. Greater detail and explanation of the deuces offense is provided in chapter 4. It has to be timed precisely when the feeder has freed his stick and then feeds the cutter when he is open. When the feeder gets into position to feed, he should have a couple of options. These options depend on how the defense attempts to cover the cutter or back up on the feeder. It is all part of the offensive philosophy of taking what the defense gives you. If the defense doesn't give you anything, you don't attack. This is a key teaching point to reinforce with all offensive players. They must have the confidence and patience to know when to attack and when to move the ball. This can be taught and mastered like all skills by drilling, drilling, and more drilling.

# CHAPTER 4

# Team Offense vs. Man-to-Man Defense

This chapter focuses on team offense. Certain fundamentals are universal to all offenses. When the ball carrier gets the ball, he should always look back to the man who gave him the ball. Against a man-to-man offense, he might be open on a simple give-and-go. Against a zone, it might be the man stretching (rotating away along the perimeter if the ball carrier is coming your way). The second option is to look inside for cutters in the crease area. The ball carrier should always consider the third option, which is to dodge if the defense is not in position to back up. If he chooses not to execute these options, he should pass the ball. Against man-to-man defenses after passing the ball, he should look to give-and-go, cut to the crease, or pick opposite. In short, he shouldn't pass and stand still. Against a zone, this option varies depending on the offensive scheme.

Team offense is based on many factors. A good offense always balances the field so that both shots from out front and passes from X are backed up. The ball carrier always moves toward the cage. He must apply pressure on his defenseman while he reads the defense. The ball carrier must change his rhythm so that he can gain separation when he is about to feed. The ball carrier should always look through the defensemen to look for cutters. The men without the ball should always move to make their defensemen play them and them alone.

If the defenseman playing you is in front of the cage and you are the attackman behind without the ball, try to get the ball so that you can hang him up in front of the cage. When you have the ball behind the cage, feed only when you are ready and the cutter is open.

Two offenses are best suited against man-to-man defenses: deuces and motion offense. The deuces offense is best suited against man-to-man. The motion offense is versatile and works equally well against man-to-man or zone defenses.

# DEUCES: 2-2-2

For any team offense, use drills that teach the cuts, shots, and passing lanes you'll be looking to attack. To execute the deuces offense, emphasize the drills in chapter 3, which introduced a lot of drills specifically for this offense. For example, when the ball is behind, the drills concentrate on the attack feeds as well as the crease bow ties. When the ball is up top, the drills emphasize the 2v2 game as well as the feeds to the offside crease and skip lanes. When you put all of these parts together, you have a well-balanced and coordinated six-man offense. The drills and skills for this offense take a little longer to teach. However, once you have taught them, you can make simple adjustments during games to take advantage of the opponent's defensive schemes.

Introduce the drills without competition and then add limited competition so players can focus on reading the defense in specific sections of the offense. Your drills should help your offensive players learn how to read the defense. For example, the way the opponent attempts to defend the crease will determine how to attack the defense. If they are zoning the crease, use your seal and overload techniques to get open. If they are playing tight man-to-man, stick with your crease bow-tie picks. In addition to bow-tie picks, other options include coma slides or skip lanes to attack.

Deuces is versatile and it fits an attack-oriented offense. Most of the shots are generated in areas close to the goal like the crease, which are high-percentage shots. This offense spreads the field well and provides both excellent feeding zones and good dodging lanes. The attackman should handle the ball 75 percent of the time, thereby *sparing* your midfielders so they can concentrate on ball possession: swarming, backing up feeds to the crease, and riding defense as well as offense.

## Advantages

The deuces offense provides many advantages. It is versatile, applies to role players, and works well with a limited number of players. The beauty of this offense is that whichever defense the opponent tries to employ, the offense has a countermove. If the defenders attempt a tight man-to-man defense, it is easy for the picks to work. In addition, the attackmen at the goal line extended are open to dodge at the doorstep to the cage. If the defenders switch or play zone, the onside overloads will be open. However they try to defend, the offense has a countermove to get open.

Another advantage of deuces is that it gives you an opportunity to use role players that you may not be able to use in other offenses. For instance, some of the best creasemen in the game are players with limited speed and agility but are great at the skills needed for this position. This includes stick protection, quick release, and shot selection with the ability to get open and score in tight spaces.

The deuces offense is a great offense particularly if you are playing with a limited number of players. Because it is an attack-oriented offense, the midfielders have an opportunity to catch their breath as soon as they get the ball behind to the attackman. When the ball is behind, they are still involved with keeping the field balanced, backing up the feeds, being ready to swarm on loose balls, and attacking the offside lanes if their defenders are trying to help out inside. Because it takes a great deal of time to teach, it is ideal for small teams because your offensive players get more repetitions in practice.

Lastly, if your opponent is not used to playing against a deuces offensive set, then it gives you a significant advantage. For example, it takes a great deal of time and repetition to learn how to cover men inside when defending crease play. If your opponent does not use the deuces offense, it will be difficult for their defensive men to cover the creasemen. Whereas, the offensive creasemen work on their picks and overloads every day. They will have a decisive advantage playing against defensemen unfamiliar with deuces.

## Disadvantages

The primary disadvantage of a deuces offense is the time it takes to implement all of its nuances. It is a labor-intensive offensive style and requires a significant commitment from the players and coaches. Deuces will pay off with benefits, but it takes a lot of hard work to install. It can present limitations if your offensive players are not strong inside finishers.

## Basic Set

As mentioned in chapter 3, the deuces offense is made up of three sets of two players playing behind the goal, on the crease, and up top. The pairs interact with one another through picks to the ball and away from the ball. The primary offensive technique is feeding the crease from behind the goal.

## Flow of the Game

In an attack-oriented offense, the midfielders are in better position to perform the vital role of their position. If they lose possession of the ball through a shot or a bad pass below them in the attack zone, they are in much better position to swarm (cover their umbrella above the ball) or to ride if the opponent gains possession. A big part of your offensive scheme is to keep or regain possession of the ball on your offensive half of the field. In the worst-case scenario, you might lose possession, but you don't want to give up an easy clear or transition.

Any time a midfielder takes a shot from out front or down the alley, he risks being beaten on a fast break because his man will be able to get the jump on him if he breaks as the midfielder shoots. For this reason, most of your shots should be inside the crease. These are high-percentage shots and you are in better position to regain possession for swarming and riding if you don't score (see chapter 3 on swarming).

The deuces offense depends on *precise timing* between the feeder and shooter. Timing the offense is more important than the ability of a feeder to dodge his man. This offense is still effective even though your attackman may not have the ability to penetrate the defense. Most offenses depend on the offensive players being able to dodge their man and penetrate the defense, forcing them to slide. These offenses are all well and good if you have offensive players who can do that. But what if you don't? Does this mean that you have to concede victory? No. If you feed the bow tie correctly, you can still get separation and score. This is the value of deuces.

In terms of keeping the field balanced, no more than three rotations of feeding the bow tie. Learn to look one way and feed another. While the attackmen work the ball behind, the midfielders out front must coordinate their positioning so that the onside midfielder is available for an outlet and the offside midfielder is available to back up the feeds as well as cut down the skip lane, if open. When the ball is up on top and the midfielders are working the ball, the attackmen must do likewise. The onside attackman should be available for an outlet, if needed, and the offside attackman backs up the cage and looks to attack the offside skip lane at the goal line extended, if open. Both the attackmen behind and the midfielders on top must be prepared to get open against defenses that either overplay them or attempt to cut them off from the ball. If the defenseman is trying to cut you off, break in and out for the ball. If he begins to overplay you on the out move, cut back in, and break hard for the cage.

# MOTION OFFENSE

The following drills are geared specifically toward the motion offense. Some of the drills can be run in separate position triangles. You can work the attack triangle without opposition to learn timing and gain repetitions. Work live 3v3 to learn the back door and motion of the triangles. The drill figures show a right-handed setup, but you can perform them both ways.

## General Rules

Although this is a high-speed offense, do not force feeds or shots. Be patient. Catch the ball on the run and look to the passer, who is playing a give-and-go 90 percent of the time. If a player dodges, he should do it quickly and to the open area. If it's not there, he should pull out, pass, and cut. If a player wants to dodge and the defense still sags to back up, then start a second rotation. If your man is still backing up, you will be open on the cut. Look for and *use* the hung defenseman. Finally, apply the backdoor clearing-out principle whenever possible in any offensive situation. Because this is a full-motion offense and requires that your players go both ways, only use it if you enough of your players are able to handle it.

## Attack Rules

If a midfielder sweeps toward you, cut and clear across the crease. If an attackman receives the pass on point, unless he has created an opportunity where his defenseman is caught in front of the crease. This is defined as hanging your defenseman. If he forces one side of the cage, the attack player will drive the opposite side. He must drive toward the passer to set up a give-and-go. If an attackman receives a pass from a midfielder, the other attackmen rotate their positions.

## Midfield Rules

A midfielder should sweep whenever possible. If a midfielder passes to another midfielder on top, he must cut and clear to the crease for the sweep. He should not roll back on a sweep because the crease midfielder is filling in and bringing his man to him. If the midfielder passes to an attackman, he must cut back door to the crease. If an attackman passes behind to the point, this initiates a give-and-go by the wing attackmen and a rotation by the midfielders. When in doubt, midfielders should cut, clear through, and rotate.

# DRIVE RIGHT WING BACKDOOR DRILL

In this drill, the feeder X works on the timing and placement of the feed. The wingman works on his backdoor cut. Although it is a right-handed cut, the player may use his left hand if that makes it easier for him to protect his stick from the top defender if he slides down to cover him. The cutter must hold his stick up precisely where he wants the feeder to pass (see figure 4.1).

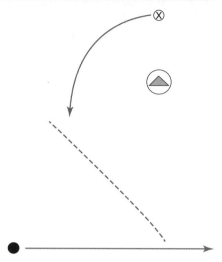

**Figure 4.1** Drive right wing backdoor drill.

## MIDFIELDER DUMP INSIDE DRILL

In this drill, the midfielder sweeps across the top and reads his options inside. He feeds the creaseman, who curls and shoots (see figure 4.2).

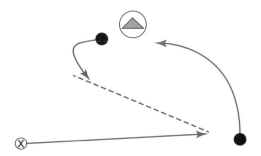

**Figure 4.2**   Midfielder dump inside drill.

## DRIVE BACKDOOR DRILL

This is similar to the previous drill, except the midfielder feeds to the onside backdoor cutter (see figure 4.3).

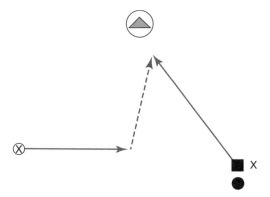

**Figure 4.3**   Drive backdoor drill.

# GIVE-AND-GO DOWN THE SIDE DRILL

In this drill, a midfielder (M1) initiates his give-and-go down the side. M2 rotates over to back up, and M3 rotates to replace the vacated area on top (see figure 4.4).

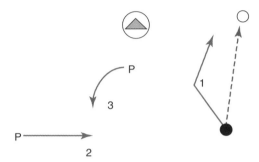

**Figure 4.4**   Give-and-go down the side drill.

# GIVE-AND-GO FROM THE WING DRILL

The wing attackman passes behind and immediately cuts to the cage. This is similar to the wing backdoor cut except that it is initiated off of a pass (see figure 4.5).

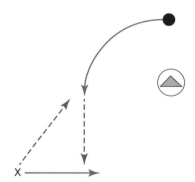

**Figure 4.5**   Give-and-go from the wing drill.

# WING DRIVE FROM THE WING DRILL

This is a companion drill to the give-and-go from the wing. The wingman clears through and the top midfielder drives the lane to the cage. The cut is either directly to the ball carrier or down to the onside pipe, depending on the defensive positioning. These cuts can be initiated either by a pass from the wing or a drive by the attackman at X (see figure 4.6).

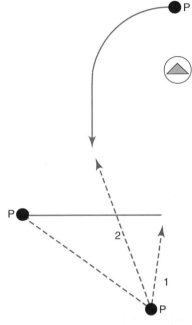

**Figure 4.6**    Wing drive from the wing drill.

# MOTION OFFENSE: PART 1

This all-purpose offense was used successfully by Paul Doherty and Kevin Sheehan at Adelphi University in the early 1980s. It can be used against both man-to-man and zone defenses. Chapter 5 goes into greater detail on zone offense vs. zone defense. The value of this offense is that you can attack either defense with the same offense you use or practice every day. A major disadvantage is that to run it effectively, all players should be able to go both ways. Because of this, you run the risk of burning out your offensive players if your depth is limited. This can be both a positive and a negative depending on how your depth compares to your opposition's. If you have equal or more depth, this is a great offense to run them into the ground. If they have greater depth, you have to be careful not to burn out your team.

## Purpose

An advantage to the motion offense is that six players will always be in motion, which minimizes backup on the ball. The crease defenseman must play off the crease, and the midfielder is forced to play crease defense. Every play is in isolation for the man receiving the ball, and every play involves a give-and-go. Each player has the opportunity to feed, shoot, cut, or dodge, therefore, feeling total involvement and greater motivation to improve these skills.

The principles of this offense can be used against any defense and adapted to most other offenses. Each player is aware of where everybody else is at all times so they can anticipate the play, which allows a team with greater depth to force the opponent's defense to perform at a very high work rate. With patience, motion offense produces high-percentage shots and minimizes double teams.

Motion offense requires depth or outstanding conditioning or both. It requires well-balanced talent because players must play both sides, and all six offensive players must pass, shoot, dodge, and cut. Because of this, it is difficult to hide a weak player. At times, a motion offense is too structured, which allows for little freelance play. It requires disciplined players. It does not screen the goalie, and it does not allow picks on cuts.

## Setup

Figure 4.7 illustrates the two triangles of the motion offense. The midfielders play the triangle with two men up top and one on the crease. The attackmen's triangle has two attackmen on the wings

**Figure 4.7**  Motion offense basic setup.

and one at X. The midfielders play all three positions shown, while the attackmen rotate among both corners and point, but never stay on crease.

## Execution

### *Step 1*

A midfielder (M2) passes to an attackman (A2) then cuts behind the defensive man to the crease and the other midfielders fill. Any time you cut, you should try to get open, not merely balance the triangle. For example, when M2 passes down the side, the backdoor cut might be wide open. But if his man follows him down, M1 must read the defense. If the defense sloughed in to go with the backdoor cut, M1 adjusts his cut directly A2. This is why it is important for the man receiving the ball to always look back to the man

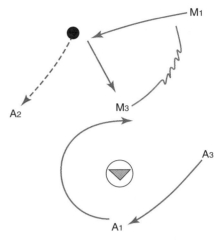

**Figure 4.8**   Motion offense step 1.

who gave him the ball. The same goes for A1 when he rotates through the crease. If he's open, he just stops and pops out for the ball (see figure 4.8).

### *Step 2*

Figure 4.9 illustrates the movement of the two triangles in opposite directions. When an attackman (A2) passes behind to A1, he immediately cuts to the crease. He first has a give-and-go option, and he also initiates the clockwise rotation of the attack. The players in the midfield triangle begin their onside cut on the same pass, thereby initiating the counterclockwise rotation of the midfielders. As A1 rotates up to the wing, he must read his many options. In addition to A2 on a give-and-go, he has M2 on a drive to the cage, as well A3 at the back pipe. On

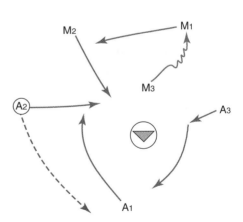

**Figure 4.9**   Motion offense step 2.

all attack drives to the goal line extended, the ball carrier has three options and reads them in priority from the onside to the offside. Option 1 is the onside wing, option 2 is the onside midfielder drive, and option 3 is the offside attackman at the back pipe. It is essential that the offside attackman poses a threat to score. He must force the defense to honor him at the back pipe. If he rotates blindly to X, his defenseman is in an ideal position to pick up cutters into the crease area. All offensive men must make their man play them and them alone. As soon as a defenseman takes his eye off of his player, the player must immediately find space to get the ball and attack.

### Step 3

When the ball is passed from the wing up top, it initiates a rotation opposite of when it is passed down the side. In this case, the midfielder sweeps across the top of the formation, initiating a clockwise rotation by the midfielders. The attack rotates counterclockwise. As a midfielder (M2) sweeps across the top, he has the same options looking from the onside to the offside. Option 1 is the M1 clearing back door to the cage. Option 2 is the wing attackman (A3) cutting through the crease. Option 3 is M3 rotating out of the crease and, if open, curling to the ball to become a threat. He also has A1, who is rotating up to the wing (see figure 4.10).

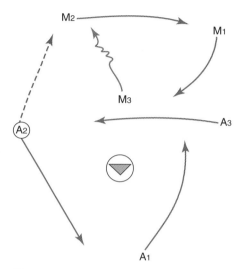

**Figure 4.10**   Motion offense step 3.

### Step 4

Any time the ball is passed down the side, it initiates a give-and-go off of the midfield rotation. This initiates an exchange by the other two attackmen, A1 cutting around the crease and A2 rotating back to X (see figure 4.11).

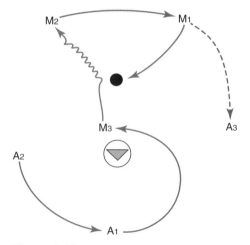

**Figure 4.11**   Motion offense step 4.

### Step 5

Often while making this move to the point, an attackman will find that he has hung his man, which means the defensive man is caught in front of the cage while the man he is guarding gets the ball directly behind the cage. The attackman must yell "hung" and rotate 180 degrees from his man. If the defenseman stays in front, his attackman has all day to pick apart the defense. So as long as his man stays in front and doesn't come behind to pressure him, players switch into a five-man rotating-zone offense (see figure 4.12). The five

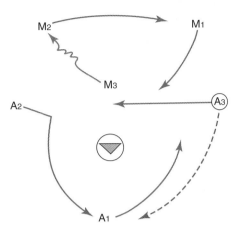

**Figure 4.12**   Motion offense step 5.

men above the goal line extended rotate counterclockwise using the wing-drive options on the left side of the rotation of the player at X (see chapter 5, figure 5.6). So long as the attackman is uncovered, his options are the wingman going back door, the drive man coming down the lane, and the man rotating through the offside crease. The rotation is continuous, so at any given point he has the three options: the wing backdoor cut, the drive cut, and the offside crease option.

If the defender goes to play the man behind, the ball carrier goes opposite to force a defensive slide. If he does not have an immediate 2v1, he pulls out and rotates into the regular offense. The ball carrier initiates the offense from X. When this happens, the normal give-and-go option is eliminated because the attackman has the option to drive either side. Whichever side he selects, the rotation begins with the onside wing going back door, the offside attack (A2) going to the back pipe, and the midfield rotation going opposite the attack. For example, if A1 drove to the right-hand wing, the attack rotation is counterclockwise and the midfield rotation is clockwise.

## MOTION OFFENSE: PART 2

Refer to the motion offense step 5 figure. Although rotating is crucial in this offense, you cut not only to create space for the ball carrier, but also to get open. When you cut, you must always keep your eye on the ball carrier and read your defenseman. If he drops off you to back up and you are open, stop and stay in the soft (open) spot of the defense. If the second slide picks you up, continue your cut to open the lane for the man that he left.

When A1 drives to the goal line extended, all five men off the ball rotate. While doing this, each one reads his defenseman to see what adjustment he can make to get open. For example, if A2, as he cuts to the backside pipe, sees that his defenseman has shifted to pick up A3, he stays at the backside pipe so long as he is open.

If the defender from up top slides down to pick him up, he immediately rotates behind the goal to back up and become an outlet. The defender up top is identified as the player farthest from the ball location.

All three midfielders, as they initiate their rotation, do so with the purpose of clearing space as well as getting open. M1, cutting down the onside pipe, is an immediate shot option, if open. M2, filling the spot vacated by M1, is normally an outlet but could be a threat if his defensive man slid down the pickup (M1). M3, as he rotates out of the crease, must know whether the defense is playing him. If they left him open because his man slid to help out elsewhere, he must immediately make himself a threat to get the ball and shoot. In summary, all five men off the ball must rotate with the purpose of getting open. The ball carrier must read all of his options and not merely carry the ball from one spot to the next spot. Each ball carrier must be a threat to penetrate the defense and either feed or shoot.

# PROGRESSION 1: MOTION OFFENSE—TEACHING THE TRIANGLES

To teach motion offense and its concepts, begin with one triangle at a time.

## ATTACK TRIANGLE (3V3)

For drill purposes, A1 starts with the ball and drives either side to initiate the rotation. He has two options: A3 on the backdoor cut or A2 at the offpipe. If neither option is open when the pointman carries the ball to the GLE, he rolls and throws back to the far wing attackman, who has come to the point (see figure 4.13).

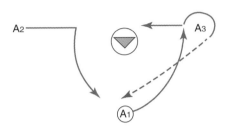

**Figure 4.13** Attack triangle (3v3).

When A1 drives the right side, his first option is to A3 going back door. If A3 is open, he slows his cut so that he can get a feed right on the crease. The second option for A1 is to the offside wing (A2), who should hang at the offside pipe before he rotates behind. If D2 slid in to pick up A3, A2 is open. If neither option is open, A1 turns and throws back to A2 at the point behind the cage. In a game

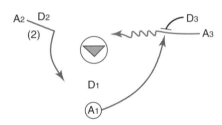

**Figure 4.14** Attack triangle drill.

situation, A1 has the option to dodge. In the attack triangle drill, players coordinate their timing, spacing, and passing (see figure 4.14).

If players understand the concept, when the attackman drives left side, they will find space in the same way. With this understanding in place, your attackmen can play offense as a unit.

## MIDFIELD TRIANGLE (3V3)

With this triangle in place, in another station or on another day with younger players, you can teach the midfield triangle from the top with a 3v3 midfield group. The first midfielder sweeps as the second midfielder cuts to the open space in the middle, and the crease midfielder finds his space away from the cage. When M1 is sweeping across the top, his first option is to M2, who is cutting to the crease, and his second option is to M3, who is rotating out of the crease. M3, as he rotates out of the crease, must be aware that he is an option. If M1 doesn't feed either option, he should roll and throw back to M3 (see figure 4.15). For drill purposes, concentrate on spacing and passing. After the midfielders get at least three rotations, they have the green light to dodge to the cage and shoot, if open.

If at any time the ball carrier changes direction as a result of a split dodge and instead of going away from the defensive player is now coming toward him, the other two midfielders should adjust their cuts and keep the same rotation dictated by the ball carrier. When the midfielder split-dodges instead of sweeps and the ball carrier goes away from M1, the far midfielder holds and the crease midfielder moves only slightly to find the

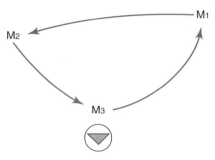

**Figure 4.15** Midfield triangle (3v3) from the top.

lane behind the backing-up defensemen. These rules are the same whether the midfielders are doing a right-handed rotation or a left-handed rotation.

With these midfield concepts in place, a lefty sweep results in your players finding space in the opposite rotation. Lefty sweep is a dodge where the offensive player turns his shoulders to the cage for stick protection and drives to the goal. If finding space is conditioned, you should not have to teach it. Try running a lefty sweep and ask your players whether they know where the space is and how they should move in reaction to the sweep. This is a good check to see whether they are simply running a pattern or whether they understand the offense.

## 4V3 (MIDFIELDERS 3V3 LIVE, ATTACK AT X UNGUARDED)

The object of this drill is to coordinate the midfielder cuts and rotations when the attackman at X drives the goal line extended. The attackman at X, if he doesn't have an opening and drives the GLE, must reverse his cuts around the back of the cage to the GLE on the opposite side. The drill should last so that the attackman drives each GLE twice (see figure 416).

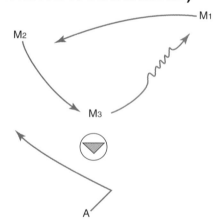

**Figure 4.16** 4v3 (midfielders 3v3 live, attack at X unguarded).

## 4V3 (ATTACK 3V3 LIVE, MIDFIELDER ON TOP UNGUARDED)

This is the same drill as the previous one, except that the sweeps come from up top. The midfielder on top should alternate his sweeps both ways as well as split dodges. The attackmen adjust their rotation and cuts accordingly. These two drills are an important part of teaching the progression of the two triangles.

# PROGRESSION 2: PUTTING THE TRIANGLES TOGETHER

After the basic rotations are in place, start with a controlled 6v6 scrimmage.

## ATTACK LIVE, DESIGNATED TOP DEFENDER SOFT

In this drill, start working one triangle rotation at a time. For example, have the attack triangle play live and the top men in the midfield triangle designated to dodge their man on a sweep or split dodge. The ball carrier feeds to one of the open men, shoots, or rolls and throws back to the other midfielder on top. Everyone in the drill plays live except for the defender playing the top midfielder with the ball. He plays soft, meaning he allows his man to get a step on him. This will help teach the ball carrier how to read the defense as well as help the entire offense with timing and finding space to get open.

## MIDFIELD LIVE, POINT DEFENDER SOFT

This drill is the same as the previous one, except the emphasis is on midfield movement without the ball. The defensemen play the three midfielders and the two wing attackmen hard. The defender playing the attackman at X plays soft (meaning that he allows his man to beat him at X). To keep the ball moving in this drill, if the ball carrier doesn't find an opening on his drive to the GLE, he rolls and throws back to X. All dodges are initiated from X in this drill.

These two drills teach both triangles how to time their rotations and find space in the offense. When you put your triangles together, you have an offense in which five men are off the ball looking to get open and become an immediate threat. Each ball handler holds the ball for as long as it takes him to make one move to the cage, read the defense, and pass the ball. All six men constantly move and make adjustments to get open off the ball.

If you have taught this progression in stages, when you put everything together you will have an effective offense that puts constant pressure on the defensive team. The slightest misstep by one defensive player will create an opening. Once your players have learned how to find space, they can use it in any offensive situation. It takes some time to teach, but when you do it in stages, it is easy for your players to comprehend. This is the essence of team offense: one player with the ball and five players getting open off the ball. Lacrosse is a team sport and was never meant to be a 1v1 sideshow. The beauty of the game is that it is a team sport; let's keep it this way.

The deuces and motion offenses share many similarities in philosophy, principles, and techniques. Both are designed to maximize the skills of offensive players and create high-percentage scoring opportunities. The teaching progression is based on sound stick fundamentals and the lacrosse IQ developed in practice and scrimmage repetitions. Choose the offense that is best suited for your offensive players.

# CHAPTER 5

# Offense vs. Zone Defense

Although zone defenses have been used for many years, they were not widely accepted until recently. There are many reasons to use a defensive zone. They take away offenses that are centered on a dominant player or from a team that has superior speed and dodging skills. In zone defenses, players cover areas (zones) so that they have more support if they are dodged because the adjacent defensive players in the next zone are there to back them up. As the ball carrier crosses from one zone to the next, he is passed off to a player in that zone. Although zone defenses can be effective against teams that use isolated dodges and attempt to dodge the short stick, zone defenses are difficult against teams that rotate men, change formations, and move the ball quickly.

Most teams have used a zone defensive package, and you must also be prepared for shutoffs either by position on field or personnel. Just as you have a different offense (extra-man offense) to attack a man-down defense, a zone offense that takes advantages of the type of zone defense you are attacking should be part of your offensive package. The basic concepts for attacking defensive zones are to move the ball, change formations, overload the zone, and make the inside shot (layups). If you have a small number of players, your best feeders should feed and your best finishers should shoot.

Practice zone offense as often as you practice your man-to-man offense. Your offense vs. zone is too important not to be an integral part of your offense. Because it takes too long to learn how to execute, you can't attempt to put it in a day or two before a game. Your opponent may show a zone at any time and your team has to be ready to make the switch into its zone offense. The biggest mistake you see over and over is when one team switches into a zone and the opponent continues to use the same offense.

Although some offenses can be used against both man-to-man and zones, these offenses are rarely as successful as a regular zone offense. When you see that happening in a ball game, it usually isn't because the regular offense works well against the zone. It's because the team wasn't prepared, and it is trying to make the best of a bad situation.

All zones have strengths and weaknesses. You want to be prepared so that your offense is able to minimize the strength of the defense you're attacking and to maximize your effectiveness against its weaknesses. You can play many types of zones. Some zones don't pressure behind but pick up at the goal line extended on the theory that they have six men playing five men. Other zones pressure the ball behind on the theory that they will not allow the ball carrier time to read the zone. There are probably as many zones and their varieties as there are offensive schemes to attack them. It takes time and effort to teach zone offenses, but no more time than it takes to teach regular offense. The goal is to fully prepare your team for whatever your opposition might throw at you. If you prepare your team well, your players will be able to handle any situation they encounter in a game.

## OFFENSE VS. ZONE DEFENSE WITH NO PRESSURE BEHIND

A simple offense that is effective against a pressure zone is a five-man rotation using basic carry-throwback principles as you move the ball and lead the defense. In a carry throwback, the ball carrier carries the ball from his zone into the adjacent zone. This forces the defenders to make decisions: Do they stay with their man or switch as he leaves one zone and enters another? Whatever their decision, it can create openings that you might be able to take advantage of. Throwback means that after you have carried the ball out of your zone, you roll to the outside and throw back to your teammate who has rotated into your vacated zone. With the roll throwback, it is important to turn to the outside because you might be pressured or doubled as you enter the seam of the new zone. The seam is where two zones come together.

Any time you carry the ball from one zone into another, your teammate must rotate away from you (stretching) as you enter his zone. If the other team tries to double you at the seam of the new zone, then your teammate becomes an immediate option. The offensive principles are similar to those of man-to-man in that you first must look to the man who gave you the ball. The second option is to look inside for the creaseman or other cutters that might be open. The third option is that the ball carrier has permission to dodge if open. Don't assume that because you are playing a zone that you can't dodge. You can dodge any time the defense is out of position for a backup. If none of these options are open, throw back to the adjacent man.

Effective ways to attack a zone are either to move the ball or move the players. The best is a combination of both. The offenses we discuss rotate men from one zone to another as they move the ball. You can either use a four- or five-man rotation depending on your players. For example, if you have one player who is a pure creaseman, you might want to take advantage of his unique skills and keep him on the crease, using a four-man rotation (see figure 5.1).

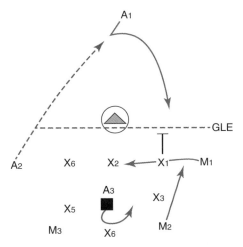

**Figure 5.1**  Four-man rotation.

# OFFENSE VS. ZONE DEFENSE, NO PRESSURE BEHIND (FOUR-MAN ROTATION WITH BALL AT X)

## Setup

An attackman (A1) is the feeder at X, C is the creaseman and is not involved in the rotation, and the others are M1, M2, M3, and A2.

If a player is used to the crease area, keep him inside where he is familiar with the soft spot in zones and the type of shots he will use. When attacking a zone that does not pressure behind but picks up at the goal line extended, he attacks the ball from X. When he has the ball behind and is not pressured, he has a preview of how the defense is trying to cover the rotating four perimeter players. The four perimeter players are rotating in a counterclockwise motion simultaneously. The creaseman is not involved in the rotation. When the attackman at X penetrates the GLE and draws a defensive slide, he must read the defense to see how they are attempting to pick up his options. His first option is to the onside wingman going back door (wing cut) when the wing defenseman picks up A1 at the GLE. At the same time as the wingman makes his cut, the top midfielder (M2) makes his drive cut into the area vacated by M1 (option 2). How the defense slides determined which options are best for A1. If, for example, wingman X1 picks up A1 at the GLE and the top defensive midfielder (X4) slides down to pick up M1 on the backdoor cut, M2 might be his best option. If creaseman X2 picks up M1, then the creaseman C is his best option (option 3). So long as A1 draws the wing defenseman X1, one of these options should be open because three players are out front being played by two defenders. The rotation by the four perimeter players is continuous. A1, the feeder, doesn't have to force anything. The only thing he needs is patience and one of these options will open up (see figure 5.2).

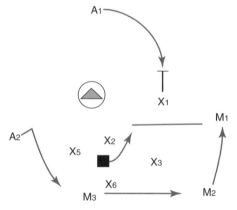

**Figure 5.2**  Four-man rotation with ball at X.

# OFFENSE VS. ZONE DEFENSE, NO PRESSURE BEHIND (MAN WITH BALL ON TOP)

When the ball is on top, players look to carry the ball and stretch the defense so that they can attack at the seams. As the defensive man playing the stretch man releases him to pick up the ball as it enters his zone, the stretch man might have an opportunity to get the ball and become a feeder or shooter. He is usually the ball carrier's first option.

## OPTIONS WITH BALL ON TOP

M2 passes to M3 and immediately tries to stretch opposite the ball. M3 carries across the top and immediately looks to his first option, the man who gave him the ball (M2), cutting down the alley into the seam (option 1, see figure 5.3). His second option is the onside wing (M1), who is cutting back door to the crease (see figure 5.3). His third option is to the crease (C) popping out (see figure 5.4). Finally, his fourth option could be the offside wing attackman in the skip lane at the GLE (see figure 5.5). He does have the option to go to the cage if the defense is out of position and there is no backup. If none of these options are open, M3 rolls and throws back to A2, who has replaced him on top.

Any time the midfielders pass the ball to X, it initiates the following responses.

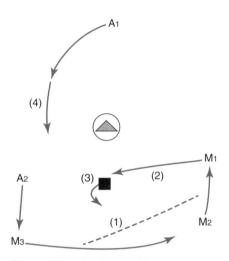

**Figure 5.3** Options with ball on top.

## ONSIDE WING DRIVE OVERLOAD

M1 passes the ball to X to initiate the rotation from above starting from a give-and-go. M1 makes the wing cut, and M2 drives into the area vacated by M1. This rotation is continued by the four perimeter players. The ball carrier reads the field and executes any of the options mentioned in the previous drill (see figure 5.4).

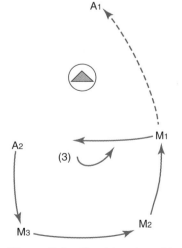

**Figure 5.4** Onside wing drive.

## OFFSIDE WING DRIVE OVERLOAD

Attackman A2 passes to A1, who immediately penetrates the defense on the offside and initiates the wing-drive rotation by the other midfielders (see previous drill). The rotation by the midfielders is always in a counterclockwise motion because they are usually predominately right-handed (see figure 5.5). If you are fortunate enough to have players who can play right- or left-handed, you could reverse the rotation and penetrate the offense from behind on the other side.

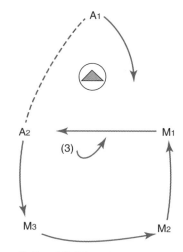

A1, the quarterback of the offense, must keep in mind that as long as he has the ball and the defenders are not pressing him until he penetrates the GLE, he controls the game. They cannot score without the ball, and the offense can score if they exhibit patience, timing, and execution.

**Figure 5.5** Offside wing drive.

Any defense that allows an offensive player to hold the ball unchallenged within 5 yards of the GLE will give up high-percentage shots. If they continue giving up, it will be difficult to come out with a win.

## OFFENSE VS. ZONE DEFENSE,
## NO PRESSURE BEHIND (FIVE-MAN ROTATION)

The five-man rotation is essentially the same as the four-man rotation except that the crease attackman has been eliminated, and he is now part of the rotation. You can use these rotating offenses if your players are predominately right- or left-handed. The figure and explanations that follow are for right-handed players (see figure 5.6).

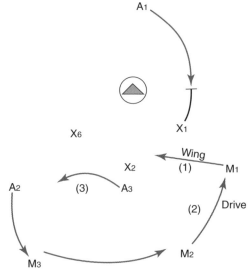

**Figure 5.6** 5-man rotation: no pressure at Y, ball at X.

## FIVE-MAN ROTATION, BALL AT X

All perimeter players (M1, M2, M3, A2, and A3) could be right-handed. It is best if A1 can feed both ways, but you can get by with a left-handed feeder. The options for A1 when the ball is behind are the same as those in the four-man rotation. The only difference is that there is no set creaseman, so the player rotating through that spot might not have the same experience in finding space as he cuts through. A1's options are numbered in figure 5.6. Once he draws defenseman X1, his immediate option is M1 on the wing backdoor cut. His second option is M2 cutting down in the area that M1 just vacated.

His third option is the attackman rotating to the back pipe (A3). As A3 rotates across the cage, he must read the actions of defenseman X2.

If, for example, X2 slides down to pick up M1, A3, the attack man in the crease area, stops his rotation and finds an open area into the spot vacated by X2.

## FIVE-MAN ROTATION, BALL ON TOP

In this rotation, the ball begins with M3's spot and is carried across the top. The options again are the same as in the four-man rotation. Options for M3 are numbered in figure 5.7. His first option is the man who gave him the ball (M2), who is stretching away from him. Option 2 is the onside wing man (M1), who is cutting back door to the onside pipe. Option 3 is the attack man (A3) cutting across the crease looking for space in the crease. If none of these options are available, M3 rolls back and passes to A2 and they continue the rotation.

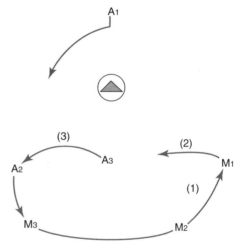

**Figure 5.7**   5-man rotation, ball on top.

## ZONE OFFENSE VS. PRESSURE BEHIND

The offense is recommended to use a five-man rotation that utilizes a carry throwback behind the cage with rotation cutter through the crease then going behind to carry the ball. It allows one player, usually your best left-handed player, to occupy a stationary feeder position (A3) (see figure 5.8).

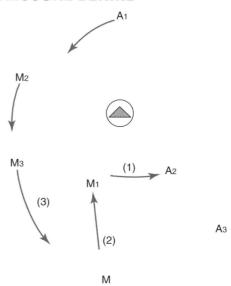

The other five players rotate in a counterclockwise pattern, cutting to the crease ball side, rotating through the crease off-ball side, and popping behind from the roll throwback to become the feeder. In this offense, the primary option is to attack the defense from behind the goal. When A1 gets the ball, his immediate option is to look back to the man who gave him the ball (M2) (option 1). His second option is to

**Figure 5.8** Zone offense vs. pressure behind.

A2 on the offside crease. As A1 carries the ball behind the cage, he looks to the onside midfield cut by M1 to the onside pipe (option 3). If none of these options are open, A1 turns and throws back to A2, who has rotated to X. All five men rotate together and time their cuts when the player at X receives the ball.

A3, out on the wing, is not involved in the rotation and provides an additional option on the backside as the players from X carry up to the wing. A3 is also an outlet for the player at X and can become an additional feeder from the wing. A3's first option as a feeder is to the offside crease (A2) cutting to the onside pipe. His second option is the top midfielder (M1) cutting to the offside pipe, and his third option is to M3 rotating up on the far side. If none of these options are open, he immediately passes the ball to X behind and they continue the five-man rotation. Most of the ball carrying is generated by the five men in the rotation attempting to feed and attack from X.

## 2-2-2 ZONE OFFENSE WITH BALL ON TOP

Teams that use deuces can use the four-man rotation as well. When M1 has the ball up top, he has the same options as the previous drill. As he carries, his counterpart (M2) stretches down the lane for his first option (see figure 5.9). As M1 gets to the center of the field (meaning the formation has rotated more to a diamond), the attackman (A3) cutting across the crease becomes his second option. His third option is the offside wing attackman (A1) at the GLE. If none of these options are available, he rolls and throws back to M3, who has rotated up top. Immediately after he passes to M3, he stretches down the lane and the rotation continues.

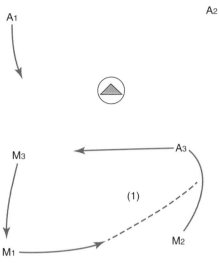

**Figure 5.9**   2-2-2 zone offense: ball on top.

## 2-2-2 ZONE OFFENSE WITH BALL AT X

When the ball is at X, the four-man rotation uses two attackmen behind and the other attackman and midfielder on the crease. When A2 has the ball, he passes over to A1 and immediately stretches. A1 carries the ball behind to X and his first option is to A2. As he continues to carry, his second option is to M3 on the offside crease. Finally, his third option is to the far-side midfielder in the skip lane, if open. When the ball is behind, the onside top midfielder (M1) backs up feeds to the crease as well as serving as an onside outlet, if needed. If the ball is passed up to him, he looks back to the man who gave him the ball for a possible give-and-go or carries the ball across the top to

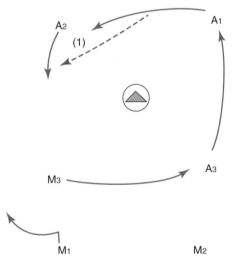

**Figure 5.10**   2-2-2 zone offense: ball at X.

begin the rotation from up top. M2 is also backing up feeds to the offside crease as well as looking to come down the skip lane when the ball is behind.

For a zone offense to be effective, it has to be an integral part of your team offense. You must practice and perfect it as part of your regular offensive practice segments. The spacing and options are basic, but you must drill the timing and reads so that they become second nature to your players. When this is accomplished, it makes attacking a zone defense much easier. What makes zone defenses effective is that most teams do not regularly practice zone offense. It is difficult to install a zone offense in a few days to prepare for an opponent that's using a zone defense.

If you don't have a zone offense because you feel that few of your opponents use a zone defense, you should at least develop an extra-man offense (EMO) that changes formations so you're prepared if you find yourself unexpectedly facing a zone. A good example is the extra-man freelance set discussed in chapter 12 that rotates sets from a 3-3 to 1-3-2 to a 1-4-1. Changing offensive sets is a good way to attack a zone defense. This offense gives you three looks against a zone, but all of your offensive players must be familiar with this offense. A good way to accomplish this is when you have Scout EMO practice vs. your man-down defense. Your offensive players who are not on your regular EMO team should use this offense against your man-down defense.

# CHAPTER 6

# Individual Defensive Techniques

Learning individual defensive skills is important for all players, regardless of their position. During the course of a game, attack players are called on to ride after the defensive team gains ball possession; midfielders are two-way players by the nature of the position; defensemen serve as the backbone of team defense; and the goalie must be prepared to face a variety of situations that require fundamentally sound defense.

Regardless of athletic ability, playing defense effectively in lacrosse can be done through desire, hard work, and communication skills. Fred Smith, longtime defensive coach at Johns Hopkins University, reminded his players, "You play defense with your legs, your head, and your heart." Note that there is no mention of the lacrosse stick in that credo. Defense is the only position on the field that requires five men to move and adjust every time a pass is made. This is why we say that defense is played with your legs. A defenseman must be agile, smart, quick, and in excellent condition.

## BODY POSITIONING

Footwork and body positioning are the keys to good defense. Your body should be low, with your head up, back straight, knees bent, and weight on the balls of your feet. Feet should be shoulder-width apart and parallel. Always position yourself between the man you are guarding and the goal. How close you are to your man depends on his position on the field and the location of the ball. If he's playing inside, on or near the crease, you must be close enough to check his stick before the ball gets to him. If he is playing on the perimeter, you should be close enough to get to him as he receives the ball. When he has the ball, overplay slightly to stick side and be prepared to run hip to hip with him. When he is running with the ball, be prepared to receive directions from your off-ball defenders who will make calls such as pick, switch, go, or bingo.

A pick is when an opposing offensive player tries to set up a screen off the ball, hoping to prevent you from keeping up with the player you are guarding. The pick call is followed by one of the other three commands. Go means there is room for you to slide above the pick and stay with your man (see figure 6.1). Switch means it appears that you are going to run into the man setting up the pick so an exchange will be made (see figure 6.2). Your teammate will pick up the man you are guarding, and you will

**Figure 6.1** Proper form for performing a pick in the go position.

**Figure 6.2** Performing a switch.

pick up the man who picked you off the ball carrier. The bingo call is special. It means that both you and your teammate will double the ball (see figure 6.3). In a trap, your teammate will double the ball from the onside, the direction he was going, and you will double the ball from the backside (see figure 6.4). If you are guarding a man behind the goal line extended (GLE), be prepared to turn him back as he approaches the GLE. Use your entire body; lead by your top-side leg to turn the player back. Do not rely on your arms and stick.

**Figure 6.3**  The bingo call.

**Figure 6.4**  The trap.

# STICK POSITIONING

When on offense, take what the defense gives you. On defense, take advantage of what the offensive player allows you to do. It is important, when on defense, not to overcommit or be too aggressive. Do not over check, but instead wait until the offensive player gives you an opportunity. If you do not overcommit, it is difficult for an offensive player to dodge you. Use your body and stick position to dictate to the offensive player where he is not allowed to go or to penetrate. Keep a stick length between you and the offensive player. This is called a defensive cushion. Play solid position and wait until the offensive player puts his bottom hand on his stick to pass, feed, or shoot. Check to prevent the follow-through if your stick was high. If your stick was already on his gloves, simply lift his bottom hand to prevent an accurate pass or shot (see figure 6.5).

**Figure 6.5** Defensive cushion at *(a)* stick-length distance, *(b)* offensive bottom hand on stick, preparing for the follow-through.

When the player you are guarding drives below the GLE, this is a good time to trail-check. A trail check is when you attempt to check the head of the attack player's stick from the backside. You only trail-check in two situations: first, when the player goes from the GLE to X (see figure 6.6a) and, second, when you have been dodged (see figure 6.6b). Always turn and follow your man so that you are in position for a back check when your man is picked up or attempts to shoot. Listen to the goalie calls, particularly the hold to turn your player back at the GLE. Use your forearm hold with your bottom fist on the opponent's hip and top fist under the shoulder to prevent a drive at the GLE or an inside roll. If the player drives to your strong side, use the V-hold to turn him back at the GLE. Always keep your stick on the stick side to prevent the player from driving hard to his desired spot. When off the ball, always keep your stick up to the inside to play passing lanes. Do not allow offensive players with the ball to get above the GLE.

**Figure 6.6** Trail check *(a)* from the GLE to X, and *(b)* when dodging.

# STICK CHECKS

The following are the more popular checks used in lacrosse. Included are explanations of what they are, how to use them, and when to use them.

## Poke Check

The poke check is as old as the game of lacrosse. It is still widely used and is one of the more conservative checks in the game. It is not likely to cause injury, draw a penalty, or put the team at a disadvantage. You keep two hands on the stick at all times and slide the stick through the upper glove hand, guiding it to the target (see figure 6.7). The target should be the offensive player's bottom hand on the stick. When throwing this check, keep your weight balanced, poke, and recover quickly. Do not commit forward. Follow through on the check to dislodge the ball and create a turnover.

**Figure 6.7** Poke check.

## Slap Check

The slap check is another commonly used check and is sometimes referred to as the chop check. Use this when you're playing stick side and put your stick at a 30- to 40-degree angle above the offensive player's bottom hand. Your wrist delivers the check with a quick slap on the opponent's stick. Check and recover the stick to its original position (see figure 6.8). As in all checks, you must keep your feet moving. Do not raise the stick above the player's head before you deliver the slap. When this check is performed improperly, it's often called as a slash. A slash results in a 1-minute penalty.

**Figure 6.8**   Slap check.

## Wrap Check

The wrap check can be effective when you are attempting to drive the GLE or are working to get into the defensive player's body. In a wrap check, the lower glove hand drops and the upper hand wraps the head of the stick across the body to contact the offensive player's stick (see figure 6.9). A good time to use the wrap check is off of a hold or anytime the offensive player has worked himself into the defensive player's body.

**Figure 6.9** Wrap check.

# Over-the-Head Check

This check can be risky for putting the team at a disadvantage, but if used properly and at the right time, it can be effective. In the two-handed over-the-head check, raise both hands above the offensive player's head, bringing the stick over the top quickly without contacting the helmet (see figure 6.10). To do this safely, always keep your feet moving and attempt this when the player is trailing his stick (keeping it behind him) or going away from the cage.

**Figure 6.10**   Over-the-head check with two hands.

In the one-handed over-the-head check, drop your upper hand and go overhead with the upper hand on the stick. You can deliver this more quickly but with less control. Another variation of the one-handed check is sometimes referred to as the Indian check because it was popular with the Native Americans, who originated the game and excelled at it. Bring the stick over your head, with the head of the stick down and the bottom up (see figure 6.11). Use all three of these checks—the slap, wrap, and over-the-head—sparingly, if at all.

**Figure 6.11**   Over-the-hand check with one hand.

## Lift Check

Along with the poke check, the lift check is one of the safest checks in the game. In a lift check, the head of your stick is on the bottom hand of the offensive player and you simply lift his bottom hand when he attempts to shoot or pass (see figure 6.12). It can be effective and rarely invites a penalty.

## Checks vs. Cutters and Offensive Crease Players

These checks are similar to the slap check because you check through the upper glove hand of the offensive player. Remember, you can only check a player without the ball if he is within 5 yards of a pass directed toward him. Most of the time, the defender playing the creaseman or cutters to the crease may not be aware of a pass. Hence, it is important that the goalie and others call check when a pass is being made inside.

**Figure 6.12**   Lift check.

# DEFENSIVE HOLDS

Defensive holds are used to prevent offensive players from getting into shooting or passing areas. Holds are effective when defending the GLE or when an offensive player attempts to back in or create a stationary position (post up) to gain an advantage. Defensive players should be confident that a properly executed hold creates a neutral position. If a defensive player attempts to gain an advantage by using the stick to stop an offensive player from getting to the goal, then a 30-second penalty will be called. This occurs when the defensive player's hands are too wide and the shaft of the stick, and not the gloves, are the force being used.

## V- or Forearm Hold

In this hold, keep both hands on the stick and form a V with your forearm and the top of the stick. The top hand is closest to the offensive player's stick on stick side. Keep your hands on the top and bottom of the stick (see figure 6.13). A hold and wrap check can be used if equal pressure is exerted. Equal pressure means that you can apply pressure to prevent penetration, but you can't apply unequal pressure pushing the offensive player away from the goal.

**Figure 6.13** V- or forearm hold.

## Butt-End Hold

In this check, keep both hands on the stick. The bottom hand presses against the hip or shoulder of the offensive player (see figure 6.14). The slap and wrap checks can be used if equal pressure is applied. It is best used on the goal line extended (GLE) when the offensive player is attempting to gain a competitive advantage toward the goal.

**Figure 6.14**  Butt-end hold.

# CREASE DEFENSE PLAY

Crease defense is essential to success; offensive players in the crease area have the highest percentage shot on the field due to close proximity to the cage. Any brief defensive lapse in this area can result in a goal being scored.

Playing the creaseman has its own set of rules and techniques because you are playing the most dangerous scorer on the offensive half of the field. Because he is the closest man to the cage and in the middle of the offense at all times, he is a constant threat to shoot and score. Therefore, it is essential that the defensive player guarding him does not allow him to catch the ball. The defender must play between the creaseman and the ball whenever possible. The defender should have a feeler on the crease man at all times. By this we mean, if possible, he should have his stick on the offensive player's stick or body at all times. If he has to slide off of him to pick up a dodger, he must always keep his body and stick in the lane of the dodger and the creaseman. The most important rule for a defensive player who is playing the crease is to keep his stick in toward the creaseman and his body out toward the ball carrier (see figure 6.15).

**Figure 6.15** Crease defense play.

This is sound defensive play regardless of the location of the offensive player with the ball. An offensive player who catches the ball in the crease (defined as the 4-by-4-yard area directly in front of the goal) normally takes a quick shot on the goal. Positioning your stick close enough to make a check if the ball is fed to the crease area normally prevents the offensive team from forcing the action. Placing your body between the ball and your man allows for a shorter slide to the dodger if he gains a step on his defender and is attacking the goal.

## CREASE PLAY WHEN THE BALL IS BEHIND THE GOAL

The offensive crease attack player is most dangerous when the ball is behind the cage. He is in a position to see the ball at all times and may be aided by other players setting up picks for him. The defensive player must always be between the ball and the creaseman on the ball side to prevent being blocked out on an inside feed. The defensive player should use peripheral vision and maintain contact with the offensive player (see figure 6.16). If the offensive creaseman is active or working off of picks by teammates, the defender must forego his peripheral vision to see the ball and rely on the goalie's call for ball location. He must focus on the player he is defending more than on seeing the ball's location. He should be close enough and ready to react to check calls from the goalie and to clear the crease when a shot is taken. Clearing the crease means checking the offensive player's stick and physically moving him out of the immediate area of the crease. This is essential so that the goalie is free to gather up loose balls and to clear on breakouts.

**Figure 6.16** Crease play when the ball is behind the goal.

# PLAYING THE CREASEMAN
# WHEN THE BALL IS AT MIDFIELD

When the ball is at the midfield, you must maintain top-side position to stay between the creaseman and the ball. Using your peripheral vision to locate your man and the ball is a little easier in this situation. It's important that you are aware of ball position at the midfield. You must be ready to back up on a dodge that comes directly toward you. When you slide to backup, keep your stick and body in the lane between the dodger and the creaseman, thereby making it difficult for the dodger to feed the crease. Keep your stick position so that you can feel your offensive player without looking directly at him (see figure 6.17). As previously mentioned, a feeler is when your stick is on the stick of the offensive player (see figure 6.18). You can't prevent him from moving his stick. However, if the pressure on the stick is light, the officials will allow your stick-on-stick contact. If you've been given a warning by the officials, then place your stick on a portion of his body and not his stick. When a shot is taken, drive out the crease attack player to keep him from screening the goalie. If a loose ball is in the crease area, the crease defenders must check the sticks and bodies of the offensive players to prevent a rebound. The defense has a 7v6 advantage, which should allow the goalie to gain possession if all the defensive players neutralize their assigned opponents.

**Figure 6.17**    Crease play when ball is at midfield.

**Figure 6.18**    Feeler position.

# INDIVIDUAL DEFENSIVE DRILLS

Proper position is more important for defensive players because they are guarding players who know where they are going, and the defensive players, for the most part, are reacting to ball or player movement. Players can neutralize this disadvantage through proper body position and anticipation of what the offense is trying to do.

A proper defensive position balances your weight between the heels and the toes. Bend at the knees but keep the back straight and head up. Your feet should be about shoulder-width apart. Your stick should be at a 45-degree angle on the side of the offensive player.

## WAVE DRILL

### Purpose
Teach proper body position.

### Setup
Players form three lines facing the coach, who is about 10 yards down the field.

### Execution
After the coach verifies that the defensemen are in the proper stance, he waves them to the left and back to the right at least three times. Players shuffle to the side (they do not hop), focusing on quick feet, and they play half-body length on the ball side to prevent quick acceleration.

### Coaching Points
Use the power leg, the leg in the direction the defensive player is moving, to push and drop-step on the change of direction.

## STATIONARY TARGETS DRILL

### Purpose

Teach positioning, footwork, and checking techniques.

### Setup

Divide the group in half and set up offensive players with their sticks held away from the body as stationary targets. Alternatively, you could use fence posts or cones as the targets. Defensive players line up 3 yards apart and start at 5-yard intervals.

### Execution

On the coach's whistle, the offensive players start with the poke check and shuffle in the direction that the coach indicates. Every 5 yards they check and continue to shuffle. They execute at least three checks in one direction and then come back and continue the drill in the other direction by moving their feet.

### Coaching Points

On each rotation, the coach may introduce a different check. For example, slap or lift checks may be used as well in this drill.

## 32 BOX DRILL

### Purpose

Emphasize moving to the ball (offense) and on ball and recovery techniques (defense).

### Setup

Set up cones 10 to 12 yards apart to form a box. Three offensive players stand at three corners of the box, and two defensive men stand inside it.

### Execution

This drill teaches most of the important offensive and defensive fundamentals in a relatively short period of time. The drill begins with an attackman (A1) at the top of the box being played by a defenseman (D1). The second defender is in the center of the box splitting the other two offensive players. A1 passes to A2 and immediately cuts to the vacated corner of the box. A2 breaks to the ball, turns to the outside, and passes to A3. They continue in this direction for at least six passes. All three attackmen get a minimum of two touches. After that, they reverse the ball and continue the drill in the opposite direction for approximately six passes. The defenders concentrate on movement on and off the ball. For example, when the drill begins, D1 pressures the ball; D2 is behind him splitting the other two offensive players. On the first pass to A2, D2 must get to A2 as the ball arrives. D1 must be in the position that D2 vacated. In this drill, the offense concentrates on moving to the ball, turning to the outside, passing the ball while they are moving, and cutting the opposite way (see figure 6.19).

### Coaching Points

This drill provides the opportunity to practice and review most of the defensive fundamentals you will use in a game. First and foremost is proper defensive position both on and off the ball. When the defensive player approaches the offensive player with the ball or is about to gain possession of the ball, he must be under control to prevent being dodged by the ball carrier. This is where you concentrate on proper stick position as well as footwork and body position. In this drill, you are either playing the ball or splitting the two remaining offensive players. The man playing the ball exercises the proper defensive communication. This is called the defensive vernacular. The defender playing the man with the ball calls out "ball, ball, ball." All defensive calls are one-syllable words repeated three times. The defender who is backing up the ball and splitting the two offensive players in the drill calls "back, back, back." When a pass is made to an adjacent player, the two defenders switch places immediately. The man who is playing the ball must recover by turning in the direction that the pass was made, and he becomes the backer in this drill. The other defender, who was the backer, is the player on the ball. The emphasis is on quick movement on and off the ball and on maintaining proper footwork, body position, and stick position. This drill helps refine the defensive skills necessary for individual and team defense. The defender in the off position (backup) must be in position to get to his man as he receives the ball. In doing so, he is in proper position to take advantage of errors made by the man receiving the ball, including an errant pass to the inside or the offensive player catching the ball and pulling his stick in front of his face, leading to a possible advantage on a face dodge.

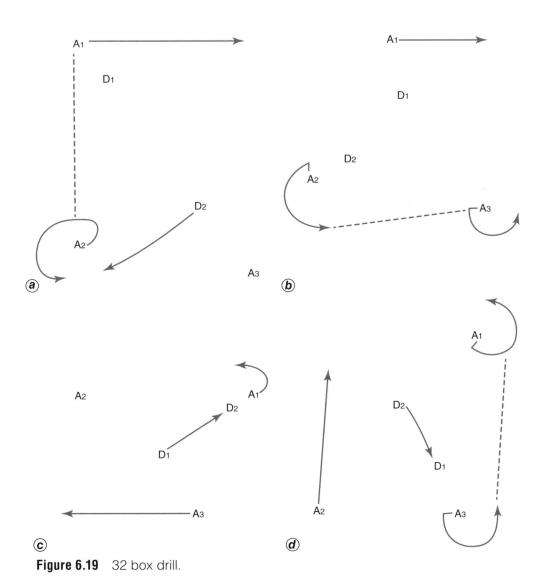

**Figure 6.19**   32 box drill.

# V-SHUFFLE DRILL

## Purpose

Emphasize both offensive and defensive techniques.

## Setup

A line of attackmen go 1v1 against defensemen. Designate an area approximately 10 yards wide and 30 to 40 yards long.

## Execution

The attackmen carry the ball and move at a 45-degree angle from the side of the zone. When they get to other side of the drill area, they plant and roll-dodge the opposite way. The offensive player is free to change direction at any time to react to an overplay. The defensive player must constantly maintain good position half a step ahead of the offensive player. The defensive player practices his shuffle footwork (on his toes, sidestepping) and can also practice his checks and holds. The defensive player must always be in position to prevent the offensive player from pulling the stick across his body (face dodge).

## Coaching Points

Start the drill at 25 percent speed, and gradually increase to 50 percent, 75 percent, and 100 percent. At slower speeds, emphasize proper technique. When the ball carrier changes direction, he must practice his drop step, the use of the power leg, and stick control while working to get a half step ahead of his man. The offensive player is free to stutter-step, roll-dodge, or split-dodge so long as he does it in the designated 10-yard-wide area (see figure 6.20).

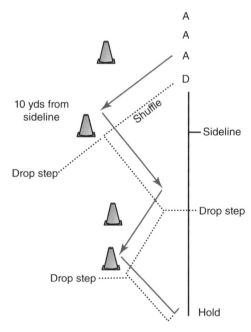

**Figure 6.20** V-shuffle drill.

# 1V1 DEFENSIVE DRILLS

These drills reinforce the fundamentals that were part of the individual defensive drills.

## 1V1 WITHOUT STICKS DRILL

### Purpose

Highlight proper footwork and positioning.

### Setup

A line of attackmen go 1v1 against defensemen. Designate an area approximately 10 yards wide and 30 to 40 yards long.

### Execution

The player's body is balanced over a wide base on the balls of the feet and should be lower than the offensive player's body and half a step ahead in the direction the offensive player is moving. If the offensive player changes direction, the defensive player plants and pivots off of the upfield foot and drop-steps so he can stay ahead of his man. The player stays close enough to the man he is guarding that his backhand can touch the other player's hip.

### Coaching Points

Remind players that they play defense with their legs and feet, not their sticks.

## 1V1 WITH STICKS, NO CHECKING DRILL

### Purpose

Emphasize all of the above but add stick positioning.

### Setup

The defensive player positions his stick ahead of the man he is guarding, on the offensive player's stick side, slightly above his bottom hand. Movement begins on the coach's whistle.

### Execution

Players work on controlling the stick so that the head remains steady and does not wave back and forth. They position the stick to prevent the ball carrier's follow-through should he attempt to pass or shoot.

### Coaching Points

When the ball carrier changes direction, in addition to using proper footwork, the defenseman brings the stick to stick side in one quick movement maintaining the same stick angle and position.

# 1V1 WITH STICKS, CHECKING ALLOWED DRILL

## Purpose

Introduce the proper defensive breakdown by the defensive players and the recovery and dropping back to cut off the defensive breakout by the offensive players.

## Setup

Players line up in pairs of attackers and defenders and move on the coach's whistle.

## Execution

Defensemen should not overcheck. In individual defense, as in team defense, players take what the offense gives them. A player should not check if his offensive man doesn't give him anything to check. If there is nothing to check, players continue to play their position and keep the head of their stick on the bottom glove that is holding the stick.

## Coaching Points

Encourage only the lift check, the poke check, and the prevention of the follow-through if the ball carrier tries to feed or shoot.

# WEAK HAND DRILL

## Purpose

Teach defensive players to force the offensive players to use their weak hand.

## Setup

Players line up in pairs of attackers and defenders and move on the coach's whistle.

## Execution

You may introduce the trail check as the offensive man plants and turns to go in the direction of his weak hand. In the trail check, the player checks the head of the offensive player's stick if it is hanging as he plants to turn weak side. The defender does this as he plants his onside foot as he prepares for his drop step during his change of direction.

## Coaching Points

Encourage defensive players to take away the strengths of their opponent.

# TEACHING POINTS

The following guidelines are from the "Defenseman's Bible," courtesy of The USILA Coaches Kit.

1. Keep body and feet moving.

2. Keep stick on stick side of offensive player.

3. Use your field sense to identify the areas that are most advantageous for checks to be thrown. Do not create offense. This means to play under control and use sound fundamentals in body and stick positioning.

4. Keep stick in front not side by side, equal, or above the hips. Do not allow offensive player to get into your hips. Use the length of your stick to create distance.

5. Do not telegraph the check. Quick check and return stick to original position.

6. Do not overcheck. The quality of checks is more important than the quantity of checks.

7. Keep the check under control. The force and power come from your forearms and wrist. A long delivery time will allow the offensive player to react and dodge away or create a foul by the exaggerated motion.

8. Listen to your goalie, particularly on hold and check calls.

9. When playing off-ball defense, maintain a defensive triangle position: man–back–lane. Play slightly to the ball side so you gain a step as he cuts toward the ball. If he cuts away from the ball, the pass must go over your head, which leaves you in good position to intercept or check his stick. Stand in a position where you can use your peripheral vision to slide, double-team, or step to your man as he receives a pass.

10. Constant communication is essential to individual and team success. Calls are made by the goalie to move players into correct positions. They are also made by individual players backing up the ball. This includes the pick: go, switch, and bingo. The examples of the goalie calls would be ball position, hold, and check calls.

11. Be physical when sliding with the body, stay square to your opponent, and prevent further progress toward the goal.

12. If your opponent successfully dodges you, recover by chasing and trailing the back elbow to be in position to throw a check when he attempts to pass, feed, or shoot.

13. After your opponent passes the ball, recover by stepping away from him into your defensive triangle position. This allows you to be in a backer slide position with your stick in the passing lane. Look in the direction of the thrown pass; do not turn your back on the ball or your man.

14. If the ball is out front, you should be positioned above the goal line extended; if the ball is behind, drop lower to the crease area.

15. Use communication to avoid switches when possible. Switching may create a potential mismatch. Always maintain position between your man and the goal; this will prevent the pick-and-roll play.

16. When the ball is loose in the crease area, check sticks and bodies to allow the extra defensive player (goalie) to play the loose ball or rebound.

17. When the defensive team has gained possession, become active in the clearing game by breaking out to the corners or getting up the field.

The defensive principles outlined throughout the chapter focus on individual, group, and team play. These are essential principles for all players, regardless of position. Defensive excellence in lacrosse relies on playing with your head, legs, and heart. Mastering these techniques can develop outstanding defensive players.

# CHAPTER 7

# Team Defense

Team defense is one of the most important aspects of the game. Defense wins championships. It is also a part of the game in which coaching is crucial. You can teach the skills necessary for an effective defense in a much shorter amount of time than those for offense. The skills required for team defense include conditioning, discipline, hustle, communication, and an overall understanding of defensive concepts. These skills can be taught and learned effectively if all of the players are willing to work hard and execute. This is where a good team can outperform a team that might be more experienced and more skilled. This is the essence of team sports, developing a group that, when working together is able to exceed their expectations.

The object of team defense is not only to prevent the opposition from scoring, but also to get the ball back. To do this, the defense should be aggressive and pressure the ball whether they are playing man to man or zone. Do not be afraid to make a coverage mistake. A good defense will back up quickly to cover slides. Each player in this system must work hard to master the individual skills necessary for good team defense.

Players must perfect and execute the skills discussed in chapter 6. To have an effective team defense, you have to put all the individual skills together to complete the team defense. The techniques of a sound team defense are the same regardless of the offense you are defending. The defender playing the ball carrier always pressures the ball. He is not necessarily trying to take the ball away from the ball carrier, but he pressures him to disrupt his timing. However, if the defender is dodged, he must follow his man on the back shoulder so he is in position for a back check should the ball carrier attempt to shoot or feed.

# MAN–BALL–LANE DEFENSIVE TRIANGLE

The man adjacent to the ball carrier always plays the same technique and has three responsibilities at all times. He is in the triangle so that he can accomplish the following:

1. Be in position to get his man if the ball gets to him (man)
2. Back up the ball carrier (ball, or back)
3. Position his stick in the passing lane to the second man from the ball (lane)

It's important that the defender gets to his man as the ball gets there. If the man he is responsible for is too far out, it's more important for him to be in a position to cut off the passing lane. His body position should always be body out (toward the man he is responsible for), stick in (in the passing lane). To accomplish this, he must swivel his head back and forth so he can monitor the man he is covering, the ball carrier, and the passing lane. This is called the man–ball–lane defensive triangle.

The two defensive players who are farthest from the ball are in position to be the second slide if either the creaseman or adjacent defender goes to back up. How far they slide in and who covers the crease depends on the offensive set they are defending. It is important that all defensive players communicate at all times. Without communication, it is difficult to keep players working together as a team. Emphasize this in all drills at all times. A player who doesn't communicate makes it difficult for his teammates to react. Normally, the man farthest from the ball is the man helping out on the crease, but this can change quickly as players move and rotate. The aim of a good defense is to take away the individual dodger, back up the ball at all times, and cut off all of the inside passing lanes. The positioning of the defensive players creates a strong perimeter of bodies (for slides) and sticks (to deny passing lanes).

# UNSETTLED SITUATIONS

Unsettled situations could occur anytime the offense gains possession of a loose ball. Communication by the goalie is important because he will probably be the first to recognize the situation. On his call to drop in, the defense must immediately drop into the defensive zone. On a hold call by the goalie, players should turn ball side and pick up their men from the inside out. Their first priority is to stop the ball. Their objective is to prevent inside shots and for the men adjacent to the ball to position themselves in that defensive triangle: man, ball (or back), lane. They want to force as many passes around the perimeter as possible. This is one of the situations in which the defense does not pressure the ball aggressively. Their aim is to slow the offense and allow their defenders to fall in and balance off the defense.

Drop in    Turn ball side    Stop the ball    Position sticks in passing lane

## TRANSITION DEFENSE

Transition defense occurs when the defense must recover and they're at a numerical disadvantage. It might have resulted from a fast break or an unsettled situation in which the defense was spread out and the offense gained possession of the ball. Any time this happens, the defense must recover and retreat to the defensive area, referred to as the defensive hole, which extends about 8 yards above the goal line extended and about 5 yards out from the center of the goal. The two low defensemen must recover to these locations and form the initial base of the triangle or box, depending on the situation. The top men in the box initially fall into an area 10 to 12 yards from the goal line extended. The defensemen fall into these areas and then pick up the ball from the inside out, meaning they fall into the defensive hole and then step out to pick up the ball carrier. For example, if you are in a 4v3 situation, the point man in the triangle initially sets up at about 12 yards from the goal, then steps up to stop the ball. He would be about 15 yards above the goal line extended, forcing the pass from the ball carrier, who is about 17 yards from the goal.

Transition defense is all about stopping the initial advance of the ball and forcing as many perimeter passes as possible. The defense must prevent diagonal (skip) passes. Defensemen must not overcommit and must be ready to recover quickly to take away the inside skip-lane passes.

# DEFENSE VS. 4V3 FAST BREAK DRILL

## Purpose

This technique is used whenever possible, including sliding situations

## Setup

In a traditional 4v3 break against the L-formation by the offense, the defense initially sets up the triangle as shown in figure 7.1.

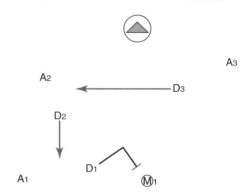

**Figure 7.1**   4v3 fast break drill.

## Execution

D1 falls in and then steps out to stop M1 at about 17 yards out. D2 and D3 form the base of the triangle, but D2 is higher so that he is in the passing lane from M1 to A2. His responsibility is to shut down that skip lane and encourage the pass to A1. When this pass is made, D1 immediately recovers by turning to the inside and positions his stick in the lane from A1 to A3. D1 recovers to the area vacated by D3. When D2 slides to pick up A1, D2 drags his stick behind him in the lane. D3 does the same thing when he slides to A2 (see figure 7.1). The goal is to cut off the diagonal lanes. As the defensemen approach their opponents, they quickly reposition their sticks into a checking position.

# DEFENSE VS. 5V4 DRILL

## Purpose

Teach players to fall in, pick up, and stop the ball in 5v4 situations.

## Setup

In this drill, four defensemen play against five. The rules for the defenseman are the same for the regular defense whether it is man-to-man or zone. The defender playing the ball carrier stops the penetration. The only difference in an uneven situation is that he does not pressure the ball. The two adjacent men have the same responsibilities as in the previous drill, the man in the area backs up the ball and cuts off the passing lane. The goal is to force the perimeter pass and take away the inside passes.

## Execution

DM stops the ball. D1 cuts off the passing lane from DM to A2. D3 sloughs in and covers A1. When M1 passes to M2, D1 picks up the ball. DM sloughs in, turns to the inside, and covers the passing lane from M2 to A3. D2 slides up and covers the creaseman (A1) from behind (see figure 7.2). So long as players are in this formation, the defense is same: one defenseman playing the ball, two adjacent men cutting off the inside lanes, and the far-side defender sloughing in and picking up the creaseman. The defense follows the same rules if the offense sets a player behind at X. The defense sets up a box, picking up the ball up at the goal line extended. The defense does not pressure until the defense is even

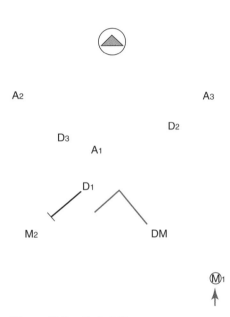

**Figure 7.2**   5v4 drill.

## DEFENSE VS. 6V5 DRILL

### Purpose

To teach the center defenseman to pick up the middle top man and to teach the defense to pressure the ball below the goal line. More detailed information about this is provided in the section on zone defense later in this chapter and in man-down defense in chapter 11.

### Setup

Position players into a 2-1-2 zone. Defend the formation following the same rules as in a man-down and regular zone defense. The drill starts with ball movement vs. the defense.

# END-OF-GAME 2-MINUTE DRI

The following 2-minute drills cover most end-of-game choose which one to use depending on the situation.

## SAMMY DRILL

If you are winning by a goal or more, you are in the *Sammy* situation. In this situation, play your regular zone defense with one minor variation. Ordinarily, the man playing the ball always pressures it. In the Sammy situation, you play a soft zone. Use all of your regular zone principles with one exception: The man playing the ball plays a good defensive position on his man. He does not try to take the ball away as he would be in a regular zone.

# TIGER DRILL

A 2-minute defense when you are behind by a goal or more is called tiger. In this situation, you aggressively attempt to force a turnover. You can use several techniques depending on the situation. *Fire* is when you pressure the ball aggressively, attempting to force a turnover. The two adjacent men deny their men (prevent them from getting the ball). The three remaining defensive players form a triangle behind the ball and fulfill various assignments depending on the formation they are facing. The triangle could be inverted, with the two men at the base of the triangle closest to the ball. The single player at the apex of the triangle is the farthest from the ball. In a regular triangle, the single player is closest to the ball. In a *tiger* situation use the inverted triangle because it puts the defenders at the base in a better position to cut off the passing lanes. When you double the ball, it is called a *bingo*. If the double comes from the onside, the direction that the ball carrier is moving, the man doubling attempts to force the ball carrier to turn back. The defender playing the ball must come around for a back check. If the double comes from the backside, the defender playing the ball must step up and turn the ball carrier back. Communication is important, and the off-man, the player doubling the ball, makes the call. Anytime you double the ball, whether it is coming from the front or the back, it is called bingo.

### Variation: Bingo From a Dead-Ball Situation

In this situation, your two short sticks play the adjacent men and deny them the ball. This allows you two long poles for the bingo and two long poles to cut off passing lanes. Doubling the ball involves a combination of a fire situation along with a bingo call. How you double and where you double depends on the offensive formation as well as the location of the ball.

The following scenarios use the tiger defense against certain offensive sets.

### Variation: Tiger Below the Goal Line Extended vs. Circle

In this formation, when the offense does not have anyone on the crease, the goalie doubles the ball. The two adjacent men deny the ball to the players they are guarding. The other two defenders would help slough into the passing lanes of the offensive players farthest from the ball. The lone defender at the top of the triangle would be helping by moving to the crease and would be in the passing lane to the player farthest from the ball. Determine the doubling technique, bingo or fire, based on the direction of the ball carrier being doubled.

### Variation: Tiger Below the Goal Line Extended vs. 1-3-2

When there is a creaseman, the goalie plays him, releasing that defender to double the ball. The adjacent men deny their man the ball. The two farthest defenders in the inverted triangle slough down to the crease but in the passing lanes to the second men away from the ball. The goalie should be between the creaseman and the ball when it's at X.

When the ball is on the wing, the goalie stays on the creaseman, but he must be prepared for shots on goal. If the ball carrier you are doubling gets the ball through the lane, the rotation is as follows: The onside man who was denying his man the ball continues the same technique. The offside man (X6) who was denying the ball must rotate quickly to the ball and deny the adjacent man. The offside crease defender (X5) slides to pick up the ball. The two defenders, who were doubling the ball, slough to the crease. X4, who is on the crease, becomes the point man in the triangle. The defense stays in the fire situation until they are reset and balanced. At this time, they reapply the double with X4 becoming the bingo man.

The rules for recovery on successful skip-lane passes are the same for 2-1-3 and 2-3-1 sets.

## Variation: Tiger Below the Goal Line Extended vs. 2-2-2

In a formation with two creasemen, such as a 2-2-2 or 1-4-1, the onside crease defender doubles the ball. The goalie helps against the onside crease against the attackmen. The onside crease defenders split the two creasemen favoring ball side. The offside crease defenders split the offside crease and the midfielder on the top side. The crease defender plays behind the creaseman but close enough to check the creaseman and yet still be able to slide out to the top-side midfielder

Against a 2-2-2 set, if the overpass is made, the two adjacent defenders continue to deny. For example, if A2 overpasses to M2, X4 slides out to cover M2. X6 slides to cover the onside crease, and X2 slides to the crease and released X6 to double M2. Most teams do not use this formation when trying to hold the ball out because it makes it easier for the defense to deny adjacent passes and force long over-the-top passes.

## Variation: Bingo Above the Goal Line Extended

When you set up a double above the GLE, the man doubling the ball is the point man in the triangle. Start out in a fire situation in which you pressure the ball and deny the adjacent offensive players. The other three defensemen form a triangle below the ball carrier. The point man in the triangle is the bingo man, and the two defenders in the base of the triangle cut off the passing lanes to the second men away from the ball.

## Variation: Bingo Above the Goal Line Extended vs. Circle

When the ball is on top, the double comes from the point man in the triangle (X5). The adjacent men (X2 and X4) deny their men the ball. The two farthest defensemen (X4 and X3) deny the skip lanes.

## Variation: Bingo Above the Goal Variation: Line Extended vs. 1-3-2

Against a 1-3-2, the same bingo (double team) situation applies. X5 doubles the ball, the two adjacent men deny their men the ball, X4 is in the skip lane from M1 to M3, and X3 covers the creaseman. In a tiger situation above the GLE, lead the farthest offensive player away from the ball, below GLE uncovered.

### Variation: Bingo Above the Goal Line Extended vs. 2-2-2

Against a 2-2-2, apply the same defense as against a 1-2-3: X5 bingos the ball, X2 and X6 deny adjacent men, and X3 and X4 play the creasemen.

### Variation: Deny Defense (500 Series)

In this situation your aim is to take away the best feeder, scorer, or playmaker. Use a number call for this series. For example, if you want to cut off your opponent's best player, number 12, call 512:500 means you will play a five-man zone against their five remaining players, and 12 is the number of the player that will be cut off. In most situations you will be able to lock off this player with a short-stick midfielder. Even if the denied player gets the ball on a dead-ball or back-line situation, you pressure him to dodge and force him into a bingo or trap situation. A trap is allowing the offensive player to carry the ball to an area where he can be easily double teamed. Traps will be discussed later in the book.

The 500 series defense forces teams to change their offense and play without their best player. They probably haven't worked on this in practice very often. You, on the other hand, can work on 6v5 defense every day. If this forms the basis of your zone defense, you will be comfortable in a five-man zone. The deny defense, or 500 series, lets you go against 5v5.

# DEFENSIVE CALLS

Defensive calls are usually made by the goalie to set the defensive scheme.

### Variation: White

White is a traditional man-to-man defense. You pressure the ball and keep sticks in the passing lane. As mentioned earlier, you need to be in position to back up the ball and make the second and third slide. The crease defensemen keep their bodies out toward the ball and their sticks in toward their man, and they front the ball. When the ball is in front of the cage, the close defenseman should be in front, above the GLE. When the ball is behind the cage, midfielders should be down low in the crease area. The men adjacent to the ball must be in position to back up on perimeter slides, cut off the passing lane to the second man from the ball, and be in position to pressure their man if the ball is thrown to them.

Defensive players should recognize the following sets:

1-3-2

2-1-3

2-2-2

1-4-1

Circle

3-3

## Variation: Blue

Blue is a combination of man-to-man and zone defense. Use the blue call with your long-stick defensive midfielder. With this defense, the man playing the ball pressures the ball. The two adjacent defenders deny the pass on their side. The remaining three players are in a triangle zone. If any of the offensive players cut or change positions, the rules are the same. If you are playing the adjacent man to the ball, you cut him off and deny the ball. If you are not playing the adjacent man, recover and drop into your triangle zone. Play this defense only for short durations on a predetermined call. For example, blue 2 means you jump into this defense after the second pass has been made. The three players in the triangle zone must help out in the passing lanes and be prepared to slide.

## Variation: Black

Black is a regular, six-man zone defense.

## Variation: Red Dog

In this situation, double team the ball on the end line with two defensemen against an incoming offensive player after stoppage of play. This usually occurs after a shot, when the opposing player gets the ball at the end line behind the cage. On a double team, the aim is to line up at 45-degree angles to the left and right of the incoming attackmen. The aim is to keep from getting beaten to the outside and to force the attackman to the middle where you can use your sticks and bodies to trap him. You must give him 5 yards, but use stick extension to poke the bottom hand and put pressure on his follow-through. The men playing off the ball should deny their men by using the defensive triangle (man–ball–lane). It is essential that all men off the ball execute the deny technique correctly. Those denying their men must prevent inside or backdoor cuts. If they have to give up anything, it should be an outside perimeter cut. The goaltender will play an attackman, but he must be cautious not to take himself too far from the goal. This play depends on the element of surprise. The defense should make a turnover within 3seconds. If the offense makes a successful pass, the defenseman playing that man must pressure the ball. The two adjacent men continue to deny their men and all others release their men and fall back into the defensive hole.

# NYIT PRESSURE ZONE DEFENSE

I feel that our zone defense at New York Institute of Technology was one of the biggest factors leading to the success of our program. When I first started to use the backer zone, I was told that it couldn't be done at that level. I saw how successful it was at some of the top high school programs on Long Island. Ward Melville, Garden City, Farmingdale, and Lynbrook High Schools were all successful programs using zone defense.

For a time, zone defense was outlawed in the NBA. One day the same may happen with lacrosse. Until it does, I will be a main advocate for its use. The key to all good defenses is to execute sound fundamentals, whether playing man to man or zone. The only thing I recommend is that if you are using a zone, you should apply maximum pressure on the ball carrier. This zone allows you to be aggressive on the ball and yet be able to support if the defender is dodged. Once a defender is dodged, it becomes a trapping situation, where you have an opportunity to double the ball with the backer upfront and the dodged defender behind. It also takes a lot of pressure off of a defender because anytime he is dodged, he will have immediate support. We tell our pressure defenders that they only have two responsibilities: either take the ball away or get dodged. They are never reprimanded for being dodged if they follow up the dodger aggressively. Players become confident when they are allowed to pressure their man as long as they don't violate the fundamentals. This also gives you an opportunity to play more players because defensemen must be substituted more often. This allows you to have fresh defensemen pressuring the offensive players at all times. The more players you involve in your game plan, the better it will be for your team.

It is amazing to me how few teams develop a regular zone offense. Most teams try to adjust their regular man-to-man offense, but they are not effective against a zone. Most man-to-man offenses are predicated on penetrating the defense and forcing a slide, then dumping the ball to the open man. In our defense, the man doubling or backing up the ball is not assigned to cover a man. When he slides to double the ball, there is no open man. This zone is all about taking away what man-to-man offenses normally want to do, such as dodge down the alley. Our defense keeps pressure on the ball, takes away the alley dodge, and forces the dodger to the inside. When the offensive player takes what he thinks is an inside dodge, we immediately double the ball and force him into a trap situation.

# ZONE POSITIONING VS. 1-3-2

### Midfielders

Two short-stick midfielders play at the top of the zone, and their job is to pressure the ball as it comes into the offensive zone. They must force the ball to the inside of the field. If their man carries the ball across the zone, then the adjacent short-stick defender doubles the ball at the seam (the seam vs. a two-man front is in the middle of the field). When the ball is doubled at the seam, the backer covers the vacated zone. If the top short-stick midfielder is dodged and his man is going directly for the cage, the backer steps up and covers him. See figure 7.3.

One of the advantages of the zone is that you can use your regular offensive midfielders in these top spots. This is an advantage for several reasons. First, if you are limited in numbers, you do not have to have defensive specialists. Your midfielders can play this spot if they are fatigued because you don't mind if they get dodged as long as they force their men to the inside. Your opponent cannot isolate your midfielders. If they try to invert the midfielder behind, he simply passes his man off to the next man in the zone. Having offensive midfielders at the defensive end is an advantage of the transition game.

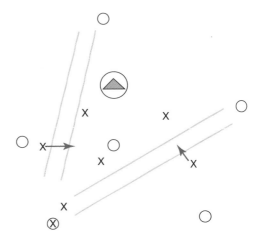

**Figure 7.3**  Midfielders' zone positioning vs. 1-3-2.

### Backer

The backer should be one of your more aggressive defenders. This should be someone who likes to double the ball and doesn't mind knocking people down if he needs to. A football linebacker type would be ideal for this position. He must also be a vocal leader because he is the quarterback of the defense. He is also the initiator of the transition game.

### Creaseman

The creaseman plays the crease when the ball is on top, and he plays X when the ball is behind against an odd set. The crease defenseman should be your best takeaway player. Like the backer, he should be vocal and a good leader. The backer and crease positions are interchangeable. For example, when going against an odd set (for example, 1-3-2), the creaseman plays the man at X when the ball is behind and the backer plays the backer's spot. When the ball is out front, the backer backs up the ball and the creaseman plays the offensive creaseman. Against a 2-2-2 formation, the wingmen play the ball behind, and the crease defender and backer are on the crease. When the ball is behind, the onside player is the backer and the offside defender plays the onside crease. When the ball is exchanged to the other side below the GLE, the creaseman becomes the backer and the backer covers the onside crease. The offside creaseman, in both scenarios, is covered by the far-side defensive midfielder.

### Wing Defenseman

Your wing defensemen must be players who understand the lanes. They do not have to be as quick as your creaseman or backers, but they should have a high lacrosse IQ because very often they cover the most dangerous offensive player on the crease. All defensive players must be vocal. Communication is the key to success whether you are playing man to man or zone.

Begin to pressure as soon as the offense brings the ball into the offensive zone. Three areas of the zone are considered all-out pressure points. Two of them are in the top spot, occupied by your short-stick midfielders. The third is by the crease defenseman, who pressures the ball at X. The midfielders pressure the ball as soon as it comes into the restraining area and force the ball to the inside. If this man carries the ball across the top of the zone, he will be doubled at the seam by the other adjacent short-stick midfielder, and the backer will fill in all vacated zones because of doubles. Anytime the dodger goes right to the cage, the backer is responsible for picking him up.

The other pressure point is the attackman at X. He is pressured relentlessly by the crease defensemen. Again, his responsibilities are the same as the short-stick midfielder's. He takes away from the outside, but if he is dodged, he gives the attackman the inside. The backer meets the dodger at the goal line extended, and the creaseman follows up for the back check (see figure 7.4).

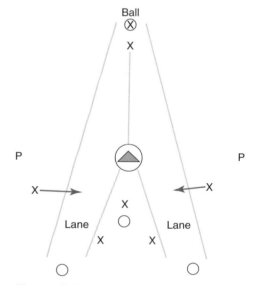

**Figure 7.4**   NYIT pressure zone defense: ball at X.

The wing defensemen (long-stick midfielder and other defensemen) do not pressure the ball on the wings. The following are the responsibilities of the basic positions against a 1-3-2 set. The player covering the ball carrier must pressure the ball. The two adjacent men are responsible for the skip lane and for their man. The backer is always between the ball carrier and the crease area. The two men farthest away from the ball have responsibility for the offensive players and the creaseman. For example, if the ball is being played by the LSM on the wing, the far-side short-stick midfielder and Defensive wing slough in to cover the crease. Only one of them actually guards the creaseman. If the creaseman plays high, the far-side midfielder covers him. If the creaseman plays low, the off-wing defenseman covers him. The creaseman's position is at the GLE with his stick covering the skip lane to the far-wing attackman. It is important that the adjacent men on either side of the ball have their sticks up in the skip lanes. Their responsibilities are always in the order of man, ball, and lane (see figure 7.5).

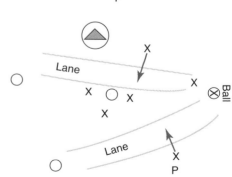

**Figure 7.5**   NYIT zone vs. ball on wing.

## ZONE VS. CIRCLE DRILL

When using the zone against a circle offense, rotate the zone so that the creaseman plays his most important feeder behind. This way all players are using the same technique they would use against a 1-3-2, with minor adjustments. For example, in a normal odd set on top (1-4-1 or 3-1-2) the backer plays the middle man on top when he has the ball. When the ball is behind, the defender playing the crease position plays the feeder, and the backer and the two wingmen play the same technique. The only difference is that the two top short-stick midfielders zone the three top offensive players. As the ball moves up top, the backer picks up the middle player up top. The rules of the defense are the same as in an odd set. When the ball is behind, the crease defender plays the feeder and the backer plays his position. When the ball is on top, the backer plays the top middle player and the creaseman becomes the backer. The two adjacent men to the ball play the same technique and the two players farthest from the ball zone the remaining three players.

## ZONE VS. 1-4-1 DRILL

When going against a 1-4-1, subtle changes in how you play are required. Because you want the long poles on the perimeter so they can cut off the lanes better, play as follows. The two short sticks play the inside and the ball-side short-stick becomes the backer. When the ball is on top, or at X, defend with a 1-4 look plus a backer. When the ball is on either wing, play it with a 1-3-1 look plus a backer. When the ball is on the wing, the crease defender plays at the GLE to help on the low-wing passing lane and to be in position to attack the ball as it is passed from wing to X. The onside short stick becomes the backer. The offside short stick picks up the onside creaseman and the offside wing slides to the offside crease. The backer up top drops down into the lane to cut off the high wing pass. This allows all your defenders to pressure aggressively with full confidence that they have immediate support if they should be dodged. You don't want the ball carrier to have time and space to read the defense. His major concern should be the defensive player who is pressuring him.

## ZONE VS. 2-2-2 DRILL

Anytime you play against an offensive set that has two players behind (2-2-2, 2-1-3, or 2-3-1) your wing defenseman plays the ball behind the cage. Your most experienced crease defender and backer play the crease. Put your players in positions that use the same techniques. For example, the backer and crease positions are interchangeable so, depending on the position of the ball, one of these players would be the backer and the other would play the ball-side crease player. The offside crease player is covered by the defensive player farthest from the ball. For example, if the ball is back right, the creaseman is the backer and the backer plays the onside crease. The offside crease is played by the far-side top short stick. If the ball is passed to the other attackman behind, then the wingman plays the ball and the backer remains as the backer. The creaseman plays the onside crease. The offside crease plays by the far-side top midfielder. However, when the ball is carried across the seam, double at the seam and the backer covers the vacated area.

When the ball moves up top, the crease defender playing the onside crease becomes the backer, and the player who is the backer now plays the onside crease. The far wingman picks up the offside crease. This is the formation you want to play against because you outnumber the opposing team six to four above the GLE. Once the other team has the ball up top, force them to keep it up top. Your short-stick midfielders must pressure from the outside in, taking away the alley dodge. The onside wing defenseman uses a fire technique (deny) to prevent the midfielder from passing down the alley. If they carry the ball across the top, double at the seams with the backer filling the vacated zone.

You truly become the aggressors against this formation. Instead of them attacking you, you attack them.

## ZONE VS. 2-1-3 DRILL

When you play against this formation, you can easily see how the crease and backer positions become interchangeable. When the ball is on top, the backer plays the middle offensive player and the creaseman becomes the backer.

The creaseman is the backer anytime the ball is up top. When the ball is passed behind, he remains the backer, and the backer drops down to play the creaseman. The far perimeter defenders still play the same technique; the two men zone the three men farthest from the ball. The two men adjacent to the ball cut off the passing lanes and prepare to double the ball (bingo) on picks or weaves in their zone.

# ZONE VS. 2-3-1 DRILL

This is similar to the 2-1-3 in that the wingmen play the ball when it is behind the cage. The crease defender plays the backer technique and the backer plays the top middle player in the offense. The short-stick midfielders play the low-wing zones in the defense.

# TEACHING POINTS

1. As the offensive player receives the ball, step to your man with your stick in front as you balance your body.

2. Stay between your man and the cage; be patient; position your stick on the bottom glove; and be prepared to check or lift his stick when he attempts to pass, feed, or shoot.

3. Set up your man so he moves in the direction you dictate by your positioning.

4. Always keep your stick in front; do not carry it at your side.

5. Listen to your goalie; be prepared to drop-step or apply pressure.

6. When playing off-ball defense, maintain a defensive triangle position: man, you, ball. Play slightly to the ball side so you gain a step as he cuts toward the ball. If he cuts away from the ball, the pass must go over your head, which leaves you in good position to intercept or check his stick. Stand in a position where you can use your peripheral vision to slide, double-team, or step to your man as he receives a pass.

7. Constant communication is essential to individual and team success. Calls are made by the goalie to move players into correct position. Examples include identifying matchups, slides, playing off-ball cutters, and stick checks when the ball is in the air.

8. Be physical when sliding with the body; stay square to your opponent and prevent further progress toward the goal.

9. The quality of your stick checks is more important than the quantity of checks you throw. Always maintain body position; do not overextend when checking.

10. If your opponent successfully dodges you, recover by chasing and trailing the back elbow to be in position to throw a check when he attempts to pass, feed, or shoot.

11. After your opponent passes the ball, recover by stepping away from him into your defensive triangle position. This allows you to be in a backer slide position with your stick in the passing lane. Look in the direction of the thrown pass; do not turn your back on the ball or your man.

12. If the ball is out front, you should be positioned above the goal line extended; if the ball is behind, drop lower to the crease area.

13. Use communication to avoid switches when possible. Switching may create a potential mismatch. Always maintain position between your man and the goal. This will prevent the pick-and-roll play.

14. When the ball is loose in the crease area, check sticks and bodies to allow the extra defensive player (goalie) to play the loose ball or rebound.

15. When the defensive team has gained possession, become active in the clearing game by breaking out to the corners or getting up the field.

# CHAPTER 8

# Clearing

Moving the ball from the defensive to the offensive area of the field is called clearing. Successful clearing results in scoring opportunities and possession. Similar to basketball, the ball moves more rapidly when it is passed than when a player carries it. However, in some situations, a player will gain possession and run the ball over the midfield line into the offensive half of the field. This is a simple clear in the true sense of the word.

### Clearing Opportunities

1. Quick clear or transition clear from the defensive end of the field
2. Settled clear deep in your defensive end (after the ball has gone out of bounds on the sideline, stopping play)
3. Settled clear at or above your defensive restraining line
4. Special situations: man-down clear, clearing after winning a face-off, and set plays between the restraining lines

To teach players how to react to each clearing opportunity, perform drills that practice the clearing mechanics used in each situation. Implement drills throughout practice: a stick drill at the beginning of practice and drills during position work (attack vs. defense) and in full-field work.

### Rules for the Clearing Team

1. Maintain your spacing and don't cut until the ball carrier is picked up.
2. When the ball carrier below you is picked up, cut to the ball, turn to the outside, and look to push the ball upfield.
3. If no one is open upfield, short sticks have the option to either dodge their man if time and room permit, or roll back and redirect the ball.
4. If no one is open on the ball side of the clear, that usually means you have them outnumbered on the weak side.

### *Common Errors in the Clearing Game*

1. Players forcing the ball into a zone or double coverage upfield
2. Goalie not moving to the ball for redirect
3. Goalie not using the full 4 seconds
4. Goalie attempting to run the ball up the field before reviewing all passing options
5. Defensemen and midfielders attempting to run by riding players on clear
6. Defensemen and midfielders breaking at less than full speed to corners, or midfielders not coming back to the ball (recut) after the initial breakout
7. Attack players not getting involved in the clearing pattern
8. Players improperly spaced on the field
9. Player failing to stay parallel or upfield of the ball so he is visible to receive the next pass
10. Players becoming impatient
11. Players violating the rules to first push and look upfield and next to redirect and change the field

# QUICK CLEAR AFTER A SHOT

To gain knowledge of the crease area, the goalie should use all 4 seconds available to scan the field, read, and choose an option. His first choice should be an outlet pass up top to the defender who is playing the shooter. If the shot comes from the wing or crease, his first option should be to the designated defensive player who has responsibility for breaking straight to the midfield line for an outlet pass. If these options are not available, he should look to his close wing defenseman cutting behind the goal line extended. If none of these options are open and he is uncovered, he can break straight upfield until he is picked up. Once he passes the ball, he becomes the quarterback of the clearing team. He is in the best position to read the ride and call out the necessary adjustments. If nothing appears open on the ball side, he will decide on a redirect or make an over call to bring the ball up on the far side. The following are commands used by the goalie to control crease play (check) and clearing situations (break, push, redirect, over).

## Check

Check means that the ball is being fed to the crease and that the players inside should check sticks. You can only check sticks when the ball is in flight and it is within 5 yards of the player being checked. This is important because the crease defender or player playing the man cutting to the crease may not be in position to see that a feed is imminent. The goalie's call must be loud and decisive.

## Break

Break means the goalie has possession and is prepared to pass the ball. His first option is to create the fast-break clear. Again, this call must be decisive because the perimeter defenders must break out into their designated areas quickly. The designated breakout player up the field should already be breaking upfield. He does not wait for the call but breaks out when the shot is taken. The crease defenseman who is playing in the hole (crease area) also waits until the goalie has possession.

## Push

Push means to clear the ball quickly on the same side of the field as the initial clearing pass or side where possession was gained. Pass the ball only if the man is open and no opposing player is in the lane. If a rider is in the lane and time permits, wait for the man upfield to clear the lane. If this can't be done, roll back to the outside and redirect the ball either to the goalie or over to the far-side defenseman.

## Redirect

Redirect means to reverse the direction of the ball from the side of the field where the initial clearing pass was directed to the opposite side of the field. Redirect is used to reverse the ball to an area occupied by fewer riding players.

## Over

Over means the same as redirect, except you pass over to the far-side defensemen. Use this when the goalie is cut off by a riding attackman.

# DEFENSIVE MAN PLAYING THE SHOOTER

This player has the best opportunity to get the jump on the riding team and to get upfield quickly. As soon as his man takes a shot, he immediately breaks upfield while the offensive player's momentum is still going toward the cage. This will give him an opportunity to get at least a 5-yard head start and if he cuts to an open lane, he should be the goalie's first option for a quick clear and transition opportunity. This is particularly effective if the shot is being taken from up top or in the alleys. If the shot is from the crease or other low inside areas, the defender may not have time and space to get open. In this situation, the designated player upfield should be the goalie's best option.

# DEFENSIVE PLAYER UP THE FIELD

The defensive player up the field is responsible for "cheating" and has the freedom to break straight, perpendicular to the midfield line immediately after the shot. The term cheating indicates that the defensive player is looking to position himself to precut when a shot is taken. He should attempt to catch the ball over his inside shoulder. This clear can result in a fast-break opportunity (4v3) into the offensive half of the field if the player is up and out, which means ahead of all offensive players of the opposing team. This would usually be the offside defensive midfielder or the long-stick midfielder (LSM). If this player doesn't get the ball and the clearing team has lost possession, he must immediately drop in to pick up a man and balance off the defense.

# CLOSE DEFENSE OR MIDFIELDERS BEHIND THE GOAL OR GLE

The close defensemen or midfielders should break at a 45-degree angle to the sideline, catching the ball over their outside shoulders and turn to the outside. If the teammate is open upfield on their side, they can pass the ball upfield (push). If they are uncovered, they should continue to carry the ball upfield until they are picked up. If no one is open up the field and they are pressured, they can roll back to the outside and either redirect the ball to the goalie or over the top to the far defenseman. The defensive players above the GLE break up the field. If they get the ball on a breakout pass, they should try to push the ball upfield. If the rider is in position to pressure the ball carrier near the sideline, the ball carrier should roll back away from pressure and redirect the ball. This is where patience and the goalie's communication are important.

# CREASE DEFENSEMAN

One defensive player should be responsible for the crease area until the goalie has possession. This will provide protection in case of a rebound and second shot. When the goalie has possession and makes the breakout call, he cuts to the far side away from the box in the area between the top of the restraining line and the midline. He will usually be open against a press ride or the attack-zone ride. On these rides, the crease attackman pressures the goalie off of a shot. The wing attackmen are normally responsible for covering the man that was guarding them. This allows the crease defenseman to get open on the far side below the riding midfielders and above the riding attackman. If none of the quick-clearing opportunities upfield or to the wings are open, the goalie should leave the crease from behind. This will give the crease defenseman time to get open on the far side away from the box.

The center midfielder or the LSM can break directly up the field while the other two defenders break at a 45-degree angle to the sidelines. If he doesn't get the initial breakout, the ball is redirected, and midfielders break back to the restraining line as the goalie retreats behind the cage. Spacing the field is essential as the clear starts to develop. Keep in mind the clearing team has a 7v6 advantage.

At this point, rotate into your 32 clear. This is an all-purpose clear because it can be used against most rides. It is also a clearing pattern off the back line.

## 32 CLEAR VS. PRESS RIDE DRILL

### Purpose

Advance the ball to the offensive half of the field.

### Setup

The 32 in the title refers to the 3 defensemen and 2 midfielders down behind the goal. Two defensemen are out wide, and the goalie is down low. Two midfielders set up at the top of the restraining line at the middle of the field, approximately 10 yards apart. The third defenseman lines up on the far side at the midline, opposite the box.

### Execution

The LSM, who initially made a breakout near the midline on the box side, rotates through the box and subs for a fourth short-stick midfielder.

The ball starts low in the center of the field, with the goalie handling the ball. He brings the ball upfield and doesn't pass until he is picked up by a riding attackman. Spacing between the wing defenseman and the goalie is crucial. The wing defenseman should be slightly above the goalie and about 30 yards away from him. If the riding attackman does not pressure the goalie and allows him to walk it up, the space between the goalie and the midfielders at the restraining line must remain the same. As the goalie walks up with the ball, those two midfielders back up toward the midline. The clear begins as soon as the riding team applies pressure. The goalie's first option is to push the ball upfield if a player is open. If no one is open upfield, he has a safe outlet to either defenseman down low. If D1 gets the ball, he looks immediately to M1 cutting to the ball. M1 cuts to the ball and turns to the outside. His first option is to push the ball upfield. He either pushes the ball to M2 cutting into the vacated zone, or A1 cuts up the sideline.

## Coaching Points

If at any time the options to push the ball upfield are not open, the midfielder carrying the ball may do one of two things. If he is being guarded by one man, he should dodge him in the open field. If this option is not open because he is too close to the sideline or might have a second man in position to pressure him, he redirects the ball back to the defense, and they bring it up the far side. Anytime the ball is redirected to the far side, the midfielders reverse their cuts. For example, when the ball is redirected to D2, M2 cuts back to D2 for the ball, and M1 cuts diagonally behind him to present an option upfield. A third option for D2 on the redirect is M3 cutting either back to the ball or down the sideline. See figure 8.1.

Although you will use the 32 clear against most rides, two others are used in special situations. For example, if you are clearing against the 3-3 deep-zone ride, switch from a 32 into a 52 clear. For sideline possessions between the midline and the goal line extended, use a sideline clear.

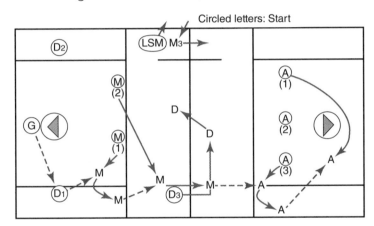

**Figure 8.1** Clear 32 vs. press ride drill.

## 52 CLEAR VS. DEEP RIDE DRILL

### Purpose

Advance the ball against a deep 3-3 zone ride.

### Setup

The formation for the 52 clear is similar to the formation to the 32, except that all players are deeper downfield. Five players are positioned at midfield line and two players on offensive restraining line. The two outside defenders go 10 yards over the midline and about 10 yards off the sideline. Two midfielders line up at the midline on the defensive half of the field, about 20 yards apart. The box-side low defenseman subs in the box for a short-stick midfielder.

### Execution

Players react when the riding team pressures the ball.

### Coaching Points

The goalie brings the ball up in the middle of the field. When pressured, he passes to the offside low defender, who draws a rider then redirects it to the far-side midfielder. Only one midfielder can go over the midline because you already have two defenders downfield. Anytime you are able to push the ball upfield, you will cut into your slow-break formation. See figure 8.2.

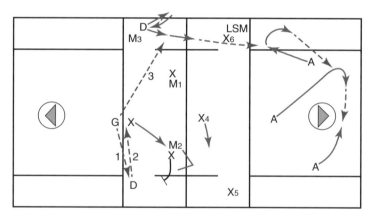

**Figure 8.2**   52 Clear vs. deep ride drill.

# SIDELINE CLEAR DRILL

## Purpose

Advance the ball when it is located above the defensive restraining line and below the midfield line.

## Setup

The third set clear is a sideline clear. On this clear, your best dodging midfielder picks up the ball. The other two midfielders line up at the midline as shown in figure 8.3. The long-pole defenseman lines up at the midline as well. All four men are stationed about 10 yards apart.

## Execution

The midfielder with the ball has several options. Option 1, if he is covered by a single short-stick midfielder, he should dodge. Option 2, if he signals number 1 with his free hand before the whistle, the two midfielders cut at a 45-degree angle into the offensive zone on the whistle. If either one is open, he passes the ball to the open man. This should create not only a clear but also a fast-break situation. If the midfielders do not get the ball, they immediately come back to the defensive side of the field. The third option is to signal for the long poles to cut over at a 45-degree angle for the ball.

## Coaching Points

If the player doesn't get the pass, he immediately comes back to the defensive side. If none of these options are open, the midfielder who started with the ball passes to the goalie. If all four players at the midline are covered, then the goalie and the far-side defenseman have a 2v1 situation on the far side. The key is that the goalie should cut upfield on the far side about 10 yards inside the offense box and force the lone riding attackman to pick him up. See figure 8.3.

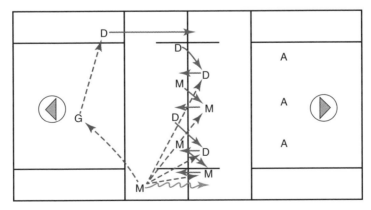

**Figure 8.3**   Sideline clear drill.

# CLEARING IN SPECIAL SITUATIONS

Special situations are identified by the placement of the ball in nontraditional locations and when one team has a numbers advantage because of a penalty.

## Ball At or Above the Defensive Clearing Line

In this situation a midfielder picks up the ball. The other two midfielders and two long poles line up at the midline as in the sideline clear. The dodging option probably will not be available because the riding team should have lined up between the midfielder and the midline. If they did not and he is covered by just one player, the midfielder has the option to dodge. If he is double covered, his only options are the midfield cut or the defense cut. If they're not open, he passes back to the goalie for the 2v1 on the far side.

This situation is nearly the same as the sideline ride, with the exception that the individual dodge by the midfielder may not be available. You don't want to dodge double coverage on a clear or single coverage near the sideline. In these situations, roll back and redirect the ball.

## Man-Down Clear

Overload the sideline opposite the box with your three defensemen. They should be about 20 yards apart with the high defenseman at the midline on the far side. The long-stick midfielder (LSM) is opposite him at the midline near the box. One attackman comes up close to the midline at the face-off X. The goalie starts in the goal. On the whistle, the LSM near the box substitutes with an offensive player. The defenseman on the far side steps over the midline, which releases the attackman at the face-off X to come to the ball. The goalie cuts behind the goal for an outlet if necessary. The ball carrier, if single covered, has the option to dodge. If double covered, he can look to the attackman cutting over from the face-off X or the offensive player coming out of the box. If neither of them is open, his safe outlet is the goaltender, who is cutting behind the goal.

> Always use the short-stick man-down-defense midfielder to pick up the ball.

## Clearing From a Face-Off Going Toward the Defensive Box

The face-off midfielder pulls the ball between his legs toward the defensive end, creating two options. He can pass to the goalie, who steps out of the goal to the side to receive the ball, preventing a redirect pass from being thrown into their own goal. A second option is to pass to a wing defense-man, who can either look immediately upfield or redirect to the goalie to begin the clearing pattern. Going back to the goalie creates an opportunity to run a substitution for the face-off midfielder or long-pole defender. Communication by the goalie is important. His calls should indicate ball movement such as push, redirect, or over.

## CLEARING AGAINST COMMON RIDES

Because of the quick restart and quick whistle to start play in the clearing game, players must identify the basic rides that are used in these situations. The goal for the clearing team is to advance the ball and create transition offense. The priority for the riding team is to create a turnover. If the clearing team is successful, getting back and playing team defense is the preferred outcome. All rides can be broken if the clearing team does three things. First, identify the ride. Second, know the scheme necessary to break it. Third, be able to execute.

## Basic Clearing Pattern for 32 Clear

In the 32 clear, three players are down behind the goal, two defensemen and a goalie. Two midfielders are at the top of the restraining line, approximately 20 yards apart. The third defenseman is at the midline on the far side away from the box. The long-stick midfielder has rotated out at the box side and the short-stick midfielder replaces him on the box side. The three attackmen are in a large spread-out triangle, with the two low attackmen near the sidelines at the goal line extended. The third attackman is in the center of the field, just above the offensive restraining line.

On all clearing patterns, the ball carrier takes the ball upfield until he is picked up. If the goalie has the ball, he passes to one of the defensemen if one of them is open. The wing defenseman has two options when he is picked up. Option 1 is M1 cutting directly to him. Option 2 is M2 cutting diagonally behind M1 into the vacated area. When M1 gets the ball, he should turn to the outside and look upfield to M2 (option 1) and A1 cutting up the sideline (option 2). When M2 gets the ball, his first option is to look to A1 on the sideline, A2 in the middle of the field, or M3 across the field and breaking toward him.

When the ball is cleared on the side of the defenseman at the midline, the ball carrier will bypass the long pole. If the clear came up the side of the midfielder at the midline (box side), he is involved in the clearing pattern. If at any time the ball carrier is pressured because of a double team or a sideline situation, he simply rolls back and redirects the ball, and the midfielders reverse their cuts. All of these passes, lanes, and spacing are a part of the full-field clearing drill, which is described at the end of the chapter.

## 32 Clear vs. Attack Zone

In the attack-zone ride, the midfielders play man to man and the three attackmen zone the four clearing defenders (three defensemen and a goalie). Against this ride, just move the two center midfielders up to the midline. The high defenseman on the far side will be played by an attackman. This leaves only two attackmen to cover the three clearing defenders. Start the ball with the goalie, who, when picked up, will pass to the low defenseman on the overload side. When he draws an attack rider, he simply redirects the ball to the goalie or overpasses to D2 for a 2v1 on the weak side.

## Clear vs. 10-Man Zone

On a 10-man-zone ride, the riding team attempts to bring the center defenseman up into the ride near the midline. This gives them an extra man on the offensive side of the field to apply more pressure on the ball. Although only six men can be in the offensive zone, this forces the far-side riding midfielder to be back on the defensive side. It also forces the goalie to leave the goal area and cover an attackman in some situations. Against this ride, bring your high defenseman and midfielder, who are normally at the midline, 10 yards down, roughly between the midline and the restraining line. Two diagonal passes will beat the 10-man zone if it is recognized and reacted to quickly. When D1 gets the ball, M1 and M2 cut immediately. D3 cuts to the ball on the far side. He will momentarily be open because the man playing him has to stay back onside. When M3 gets the ball, he passes diagonally to A1, who cuts up on the far sideline for the ball. A1 should be open because the goalie covering him had to retreat to the goal when M3 caught the pass. On a 10-man ride, the goalie can only cover a man when the ball is deep in the

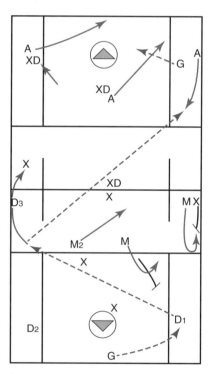

**Figure 8.4**   Clear vs. 10-man zone.

clearing defensive side of the field. Once the ball gets up near the midline, the goalie must release his man and retreat to the goal. This gives the clearing team a man-up advantage if they move the ball quickly. (See figure 8.4.)

## Clear vs. Pressure Ride

Anytime the ball is cleared from the backline or off of a shot, the clearing midfielders, after breaking out, must read the ride. The two center midfielders come down to the restraining line. The two deep clearers (defenseman and midfielder) must come down to the restraining line near the sideline. Instead of the normal 3-2-2 formation, they are now lined up in a 3-4 formation. The two inside midfielders immediately break down for the ball. They must be about 30 yards apart, and one should be open. If not, the far-side man at the restraining line would be wide open. The key on all clears is not just to run to a spot on the field, but also to react to the situation. If you are open, come back to the ball.

If you anticipate a pressure ride because you have scouted your opponent or they used the ride earlier in the game, a simple adjustment off of a backline clear is to have your best dodging short stick take the ball. The same rules always apply for the clearing team. If a short stick is guarding you, especially an attackman, you have the OK to dodge. When this happens, it becomes a dodge-and-dump situation up the field.

## 52 Clear vs. Deep-Zone Ride

In the deep-zone ride, the riding team uses a 3-3 zone ride at the midline. The three attackmen zone on their half of the field, and the three defensive players, usually two short-stick midfielders and a long-stick midfielder, zone at the midline on the defensive side of the field. The rules for both zones are to play the deepest man in your zone.

This is the most popular ride in use today. It is used because it is easy to teach and doesn't give up transition opportunities. However, it is also easy to clear against.

The 52 clear is the same as the 32, except the top defenseman and midfielder move over the midline down to the offensive restraining line near the sideline. The two inside midfielders, who are normally at the restraining line, are now at the midline. The low defensemen are above the restraining line, out wide near the sideline. The long pole on the box side is substituted for a short-stick midfielder. The goalie walks the ball up. When picked up, he passes the ball to the low defenseman on the offside. Once he draws the onside attackman and the LSM slides to cover M2, the ball is redirected to the far side. M2 has come back onside. The ball is redirected to M3 on the far side. He simply goes over the midline, and he will be open. Caution: M3 can't go over the midline until M2 has come back onside.

## CLEARING DURING PRACTICE

Clearing and riding should be part of all of your competitive drills: from 1v1, uneven situations, to 6v6. Anytime you work on these segments, the drill does not end until the defense has cleared the ball over the midline. The reason for this is twofold. The defender guarding the player who has just shot the ball must immediately breakout to get a step on the shooter. And the other defensive players must also react as soon as the goalie has possession.

- **2v2:** Clearing off of the 2v2 drill might look simple, but it's an important part of 3v2 clearing. The receiver getting the ball on a 2v1 must make sure that he cuts into an open lane so that the lone rider is not in position to intercept or deflect the pass.

- **3v3:** In this situation, if you don't get the quick outlet, the clearing unit gets to clear 4v3 against an attack zone ride. This creates a competitive advantage.

- **4v4:** The defense has a 5v4 advantage. In this situation, lock on one of the short sticks and use either the 24 ride, the 24 Yale, or the deep-zone ride. The 24 ride and 24 Yale are described in chapter 9.

- **6v5:** For the most part, you are clearing 6v6 in this formation. Emphasize the goalie's use of the crease and the midfielders getting open and coming back to the ball.

- **6v6:** In a half-field set like this, the clearing unit must react to all of the rides described earlier, plus the 60 ride and the sideline ride. Instead of having separate riding or clearing segments during practice, they are part of all competitive drills, and this simulates game conditions. Practice does not stop because of a shot, a save, or out-of-bounds situation. Immediately put the ball back into play. This keeps up the tempo, keeps practice moving, and is a great conditioner. This teaches all the fundamentals you are looking for in clearing: breakout, push, redirect, and spacing. Introduce all clears and rides individually during prepractice chalk talks.

# FULL-FIELD CLEARING DRILL

## Purpose

This is the only clearing drill offered as a culminating activity. This drill emphasizes all the fundamentals you want to reinforce in clearing.

## Setup

The three defensemen and three midfielders start the drill in their regular 32 clear formation. Two midfielders are at the restraining line. The third midfielder and one defenseman line up near the midline at both sidelines. The low-wing defensemen line up just above the GLE about 3 yards off the crease. The attackmen line up in the offensive zone in a wide triangle. The wing attackman lines up on the GLE, 15 yards from the sideline. The center attackman lines up in the middle of the field about 5 yards above the restraining line.

A coach starts the drill by passing to the goalie as a simulated shot. When the goalie yells "break", only the two low defensemen break out below the GLE looking to receive the ball over their outside shoulder. If D1 has the ball, he will pass to M1. M1 doesn't cut until D1 is in position to pass. He breaks directly toward D1, and when he catches the ball, he turns to the outside and pushes the ball to M2. M2 has cut diagonally upfield on the side that M1 has vacated. M2 receives the ball over his upfield shoulder and passes to M3 cutting down the sideline. M3 passes the ball down the side to A1. A1 breaks to the ball, turns to the outside, and passes the ball to A2, who has cut diagonally to the onside corner of the field. A2 is now behind the GLE. He turns to the outside and passes to A3, who has cut directly behind the goal to X. The first midfielder down the field cuts to the onside pipe. The second midfielder cuts to the offside pipe. And the third midfielder backs up those passes. These are the slow-break cuts for this drill (see figure 8.5).

Spacing is important on this drill. For example, when the clear is being made on the side of the three midfielders, M2 may choose to bypass M3 and pass directly to A1 if M3 is already too close to A1. When the ball is being cleared on the side of the defenseman at midline, the defenseman does not go down the field, but he clears to the middle and rotates back onside. In this case, the midfielder passes directly to the onside attackman breaking to the ball.

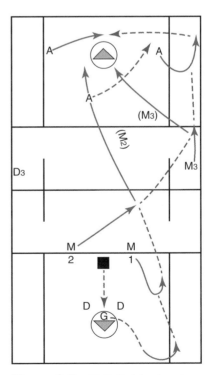

**Figure 8.5** Full-field clearing drill.

For drill purposes, anytime a fundamental is violated or a pass is dropped, players must redirect the ball and bring it up the far side. This means that all midfielders must reverse their cuts. All successful clears end up in a slow break.

As soon as the ball clears the midline, a new midfield group rotates into the defensive area. The coach takes a shot to the goalie, and the breakout drill begins. The attack and defense stay in for three rotations each. The midfielders rotate after each clear. It's important that the midfielders rotate into the drill quickly to keep up the tempo. This is not only a clearing drill, but a conditioning drill as well.

## Coaching Points

The ability to advance the ball from the defensive end of the field after a save, turnover, or takeaway to the offensive end is essential. Each successful clear creates an offensive possession and potential scoring opportunity. This is reinforced by the full-field clearing drill, which reinforces the basic skills needed to master the clearing concepts.

# CHAPTER 9

# Riding

Riding is perhaps the most overlooked facet of the game of lacrosse. This is a result of two common myths. The first is that it is too time consuming to teach riding. Myth two is that riding is an aggressive strategy that can leave your defense vulnerable if the opposing team advances the ball in transition offense. These ideas have led many teams to avoid riding aggressively. This dynamic is precisely the reason it is important to make riding a big part of your game plan. Riding occurs when the defensive team has gained possession in their half of the field, and the ride is designed for the team that lost possession to prevent the defense from advancing the ball into the offensive half of the filed. Riding is like investing in the stock market: The time to do it is when others are not.

## MYTHS ABOUT RIDING

Riding is particularly important for teams with a limited number of players. First, let's examine the myth that riding is too time consuming to teach. Not only is it not time consuming, but riding must also be a part of every competitive drill you organize. This includes 1v1, 2v2, 3v3, and up to 10v10. You should also work riding into uneven drills. These drills should not end until the defensive man, group, or team has successfully cleared the ball into the offensive zone or past the midfield line. In essence, you are not working on a micro portion of the game, but rather you are incorporating riding and clearing into every drill, encompassing the bigger picture. If coaches strive to create gamelike environments during practice, then finishing every save, turnover, or ground ball with a ride and clear is as gamelike as you can get. In a game the whistle does not blow when the offense takes a shot (unless you score), and the game doesn't stop when the defense gets control of the ball. This enforces all game conditions as much as possible. All the fundamentals you want your team to master are reiterated by finishing the drill appropriately and that includes riding and clearing.

Here are the top three rules for offensive riding:

1. Take high-percentage shots. If you don't score,
2. react and control the loose ball, and
3. if the goalie saves the shot, recover and ride.

Recovering and riding after a goalie save or defensive-owned ground ball are most important to the man who shot the ball. He is most vulnerable to being beat on a clear because his momentum is going forward. An important teaching point is that once the ball leaves your stick, you have no control over what happens to it. Rather than watch to see whether you have scored, stop and react to cover the man who was playing you. He might have broken upfield (if he reacted correctly) for the breakout clear. The shooter must make it difficult for him to get open. For any ride to be successful, this man has to be prevented from getting the ball on a breakout. Most often, the shooter can prevent this if he reacts immediately and keeps himself in line with his man and the goalie. Even though his man might be able to get deeper than he can initially, it would take a perfect pass to get the ball to him on a break.

This riding technique is difficult but can be mastered through discipline, coaching, and repetition. There is opportunity to work on this every time a shot is taken in practice, whether it is in a 1v1, 10v10, or anything in between. This not only reinforces offensive and defensive principles, but also conditioning and individual and team intensity as well.

As far as myth two and riding being too risky, nothing could be further from the truth. It is extremely risky if you don't have a complete riding package because you will give up numerous high-percentage transition scoring opportunities. You will also allow your opponent to hide a player with weak stick-handling skills or to slow the game.

# RIDING PACKAGES

To win, you must prepare your team in all phases of the game. Do this to test your opponent and see whether they have done the same. Have they done all of their homework? Sometimes, particularly early in the season, you catch a team that is not prepared for a certain ride or defensive or offensive technique, and it gives you an advantage. You can only discover this if you test them early in the game. Riding is something to use to test other teams. To be successful, use a variety of rides, or a riding package. These rides are not difficult to teach because they use the same fundamentals you work on every day in your drills. The following are examples of riding packages.

*1v1*
- Offense: After shot, recover and ride.
- Defense: Break out and get to your space.

*2v2 and 3v3*
- Offense: Stop the breakout, and play the deepest man in your zone. If two men are in your zone, play the deepest until you get bumped to switch and cover the man (if the ball is redirected to the other side of the field).
- Defense: Break out and get to your space.

The attack positions noted refer to their location on the field. Basic rules for all attack players on zone rides include the following:

*Rules*
- Ball-side attack: Must turn back the ball carrier to the inside. This is probably at or near the midfield line.
- Inside attack: Must play the goalie to prevent him from making the outlet pass upfield. After the outlet pass is made to either wing defenseman, he comes off the goalie and chases the ball carrier at the proper angle to trap (double) the ball carrier when he is forced to the inside by the ball-side attackman.
- Off-ball attack: Must hustle to the middle of the field at midfield line to cover throwbacks.

The key to all attack rides is they must line up near the midfield line and above the ball carrier in order to be in position to trap the ball carrier (onside and inside attack) and cover throwbacks across the field (see figure 9.1). These principles are always the same on most 3-man, 6-man, and 10-man zone rides. Anytime you work 6v6 or fewer in practice, you have the opportunity to work on your rides and clears. Plus, it is part of the tempo you use in practice to prepare for the intensity of the game. Intensity and conditioning are developed every practice. Anytime you work on 6v6 or less, the drill does not end until the defensive team has cleared the ball over the midfield line and into the offensive zone.

Your ride package is a series of zones, mostly pressuring the ball with the exception of the deep 33 zone. The 24 series is a combination of the 3-man attack zone and a 6-man zone. The 90-100 rides are 10-man zones.

The Hugo ride is a specialty ride. We first started using it in 2001. I got it from Sid Jamieson at the Intercollegiate Mens Lacrosse Coaches Association National Convention. It was ready made for the players I had that year. I had several very good short-stick defensive midfielders and an excellent freshman long-stick midfielder (LSM) from Smithtown, New York, Jared

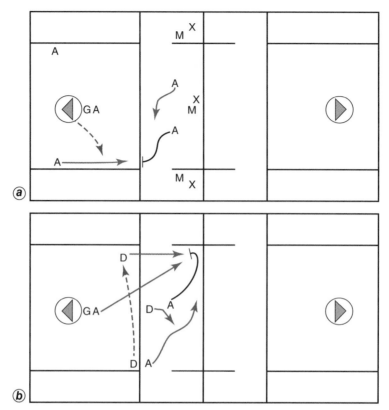

**Figure 9.1**   (a) Positioning for riding situations. (b) Rotation after the first pass is thrown.

Cullin. He was perfect for the ride: tall, quick, rangy and an excellent take-away long pole. The whole concept of the Hugo ride is to force a 1v1 with your best takeaway long pole. This 1v1 allows your LSM to be isolated on one of their long poles in your defensive half of the field. The Hugo long pole's first objective is to keep the opponent's defenseman out of the box. While he is doing this, everyone is playing a shutoff technique on their man. The LSM has the green light to take away the ball. In this situation, the LSM has the advantage, and your best takeaway man is on one of their long poles. The balance has shifted in your favor. During the four years Jared was our LSM, this was our most effective ride. In 2005, our national championship game went into overtime. The Hugo ride and Jared were responsible for the critical turnovers near the end of the game. One was in the closing minutes of the fourth quarter and two others during overtime. The last turnover set up the possession that led to the overtime goal and our third national championship title.

Every ride can be beaten. It takes two things to beat a ride: (1) a scheme (clearing pattern) and (2) execution. Sometimes a team will have one but not the other. You'll never know until you test them. Use the first quarter of every game to test your opponent. If you or your opponent has a great offense but can't clear the ball, the offense will rarely have a chance to score goals. Don't be afraid to take risks early in the ball game. Worst-case scenario: You try something different. If it doesn't work, don't use it. This is what the first quarter is for. Test your opposition and evaluate what you can use or cannot use in your game plan.

# TYPES OF RIDES

The following are brief explanations of each ride. The corresponding figures will help you to better visualize each one.

## 24 Zone

Use the 24 zone to teach the basics of riding. It incorporates the recovery from offense to defense, the cutoff of all breakouts, the pressure and pursuit angles, and sliding zone principals. The 24 zone comes from the formation of two attackmen (2) down and the three midfielders and third attackman (4) zoning at the midline. Use this ride on all shots and dead-ball clears. The key to success on this ride and all rides is the midfielders cutting off their man on the initial breakout after a shot. The crease attackman plays the goalie, and his main responsibility is to prevent breakout passes to the midfielders or defensemen upfield. The other two attackmen immediately drop back near the top of the restraining line. Their responsibility is to play the deepest defenseman on their side of the field. If the deepest defenseman is at the midfield line at the middle of the field, they both initially play him. One will lock onto him and the other will cover the first pass to one of the low defensemen. Once one attackman is playing a long pole at or near the midline, he becomes part of the midfield zone.

The four men zoning at the midline are initially covering the man in their zone on the same side of the field that they're playing on. The two attackmen down low are zoning the two remaining defensemen and goalie. Their responsibility is the ball-side man and to press the ball carrier and force as many passes as possible. The other attackman's responsibility is to be deeper than the deepest man (goalie and wing defensemen) on his half of the field. Again, his responsibility is to force as many passes as possible.

If it appears that the clearing low defensemen will beat the attackman after a few redirect passes, the four remaining riders zoning at the midline slide and bump to the ball. This is the most difficult technique to teach, but it can be done by repetition and talking until everyone understands what needs to be done. This is why you work on riding in all competitive drills, from 1v1 to 10v10. When the bumping begins, it is important to shut down the two midfielders closest to the ball. You want to force the clearing defenseman to make a pass while he is being pressured by the riding attackman underneath and the midfielder bumping over to pick him up. It's important that the midfielder who is sliding to the ball does so on your offensive side of the field. This way you have two players attempting to trap the clearing defenseman before he gets to the midline. This also allows the three remaining riders in the middle of the field to play deeper than the man they are bumping to without concern about going offside. See figure 9.2.

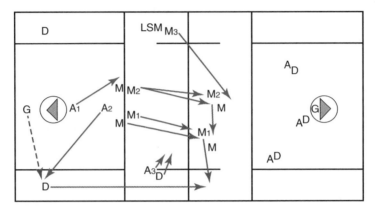

**Figure 9.2**   24 zone.

## 24 Yale

The name for the 24 Yale ride comes from the Yale lock company, not Yale University. In the 24 Yale ride, the high attackman (A3) locks onto his man and goes with him if he goes over the midfield line. Make this adjustment if the clearing long poles are good stick handlers and are beating you on redirect passes or if your midfielders are having a difficult time adjusting their zones to the clearing patterns. The Yale ride is not a zone but a man-to-man ride. The Hugo ride uses a combination of man-to-man and zone techniques. The riding midfielder must play deeper than his man but on the same side of the midline. This is similar to the 24 zone in the initial setup, except you are not in a zone but are locked onto your men after the initial breakout. Use this when one defenseman or more goes over the midfield line or the short poles are cutting down low to clear the ball. The important thing is that your midfielders be locked onto their men. The attackman playing the deepest defenseman also locks on if he goes over the midline. You are riding with two attackmen zoning and chasing the three low clearing opponents (two defensemen and one goalie). See figure 9.3.

2. The far-side midfielders must stay back onside if the middle defenseman has come over to pressure the ball. In addition to being onside, he must be in the passing lane of the attackman on his side of the field.

3. The two wing midfielders and the high center defenseman must communicate with each other to make sure that one always stays back onside. Normally, the onside wing midfielder plays the man in his zone tight and either the far-side midfielder or center defenseman will be back on defense. See figure 9.4, *a-b*.

### Basic Rules for Defensemen and Goalie

1. The center defenseman is the quarterback of the ride. This should be your quickest and best takeaway defenseman. It is ideal if you have one player who exhibits both skills. If not, your quickest player should be in this position of the zone. He decides when to come up to double the ball or when the ride is in danger of being broken. He should be as aggressive as possible but not to the point of giving up transition. He decides when to signal the Alamo call, which means give up the ride and get back to the fort (defensive area).

2. The other two defensemen and goalie zone the remaining three attackmen. In normal situations, the two defensemen play the two onside attackmen while the goalie plays the offside attackman. However, sometimes the alignment of the attackmen makes it easier for the goalie to play the center attackman. This is preferable because it allows the goalie to be closer to or in the shooting lane to the cage.

## 300 Press

Use the 300 press in special situations. This ride is similar to the 900 press, pressing the three low defensemen. When teams are substituting during their clear, press all three low clearing defenders and zone the three remaining men at the midline. Use this when teams are slow in their substitutions or have poor stick handlers on defense. See figure 9.5.

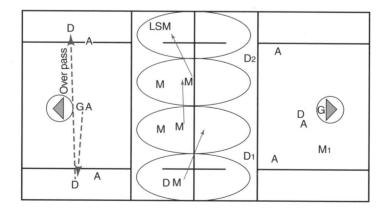

**Figure 9.5**    300 press.

# Hugo Ride

Another specialty ride is the Hugo ride. The idea behind the Hugo ride is to force a 1v1 with your best takeaway long pole. This 1v1 allows your LSM to be isolated on one of their long poles in your defensive half of the field. The Hugo long pole's first objective is to keep the opponent's defenseman out of the box. While he does this, everyone plays a shutoff technique on their man. The LSM has the OK to take away the ball. In this situation, the LSM has the advantage, and your best takeaway man is on one of their long poles. The balance is shifted in your favor.

The Hugo ride shuts off the short poles from clearing the ball and forcing one of their long poles (hopefully a designated one) to carry the ball over the midline. As previously mentioned, your best takeaway defenseman will pick him up and either prevent him from getting the ball into the offensive zone or possibly take the ball away from him. This can only be accomplished if your defensemen and your defensive midfielders are shutting off their men and preventing them from getting the ball. This seems like a difficult assignment, but it's just as difficult for their clearing defenseman to be able to make an accurate pass while he is being pressured by your best long pole. See figure 9.6, *a-b*.

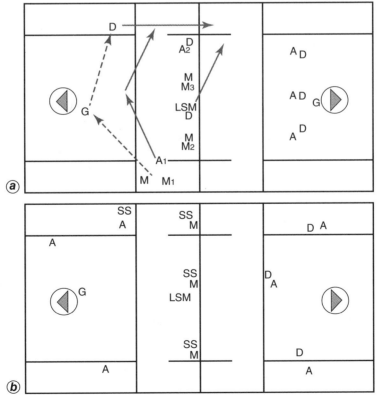

**Figure 9.6** *(a)* Hugo ride and *(b)* Hugo ride vs. any SL clear.

# 33 Deep

The 33-deep ride is a drop-back zone ride. It is the most conservative ride in our ride package. Many teams use it exclusively because it is a conservative approach to riding. It is used by teams that want to take away the transition abilities of their opponent and by a team that prefers to play 6v6. However, use it only occasionally as your safe ride option. There are two situations in which you benefit from the 33-deep ride. The first is when the opposition has broken your other rides and is getting uneven advantages against your defense. The second is when you are beating your opponent late in the game and want to slow things down.

The biggest reason to use this infrequently is because it doesn't fit into a game plan of pressing the opposition for a full 60 minutes. Your aim is to push the tempo in all phases of the game. You want to test your opponents in schemes as well as in conditioning. This ride gives the opposition a chance to catch its breath and control the tempo of this phase of the game. See figure 9.7.

It pays to have as many weapons as possible in your arsenal because you never know when you will need them. When the going gets tough, having a diverse riding package can help create an imbalance in your favor. Once again, riding is like a good investment that pays consistent dividends. The amount of time taken to teach the ride is far exceeded by the positive opportunities it will create. In summary, aggressive riding packages provide high-percentage offensive opportunities. Possessions from successful rides almost always create an uneven advantage opportunity. Plus, aggressive riding and pressuring the ball are all part of your pressure-intense game plan.

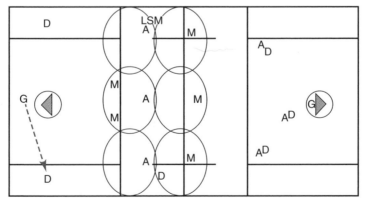

**Figure 9.7**   33 deep.

# CHAPTER 10

# Extra-Man Offense

During a man-down defense because of a penalty, use your best six offensive players in an extra-man offense (EMO). Each must have a high lacrosse IQ, which enables them to read the defense and learn to take what the defense gives them. The extra-man offense uses multiple formations, each with its own strength against the defensive set used against it. Ultimately, you attack the splitter, the defenseman (usually on the far side) who is responsible for more than one man. Every man-down defense (MDD) has its strengths and weaknesses. MDD occurs when a team is penalized with a time-serving foul ranging from 30 to 60 seconds, which will be discussed in greater detail in chapter 11. You want to attack the weaknesses in your opponent's zone. Try to have all of your EMO players be a Tom Brady in terms of reading the defense and attacking it. While you are moving the ball and changing sets, each ball carrier has permission to attack if he sees an error in the defensive scheme.

Instead of designing set plays, define options to execute as you move the ball and change formations. Each offensive set offers particular options, and you want to take advantage of the option that gives you the best inside shot. On both regular offense and, especially on extra-man offense, look for inside, not outside shots. One reason not to use set plays is that if the opposition locks off one man on your offense, the play could be severely interrupted. Another reason is if they have scouted your team, it could lead to a turnover.

The rules of the offense are always the same. As you move the ball, you must penetrate the defense, make your man play you and you alone, read the defense, and take what the defense gives you. The ball carrier should not force anything, but if any of these options are open, he should take advantage of them. If not, continue to play to the next series of options.

Each ball handler who has the ball looks inside to the crease for openings or open skip lanes. If there are no openings, he continues to pass to the next adjacent player. Among the various EMO offensive sets, the 3-3 set is the basic offensive formation.

# 33 EMO SET

Start out in a basic 3-3 offensive set on EMO. The players for a 33 set are as follows. The symbols designate initial positions in the 3-3 set and the strengths of each player in that particular position. In figure 10.1, the letters designate their initial positions.

- M3: The top right-handed player should be your best outside right-handed shooter.
- M2: The top middle player is one of the most important players in this set. He is the quarterback of the offense, one of your best feeders, and a good outside shooter.
- M1: The top left-handed player should be your best outside left-handed shooter.
- A2: The lower right-handed attackman should be both a good feeder and finisher.
- C: The creaseman should be your best inside shooter.
- A1: The lower left-handed attackman should be both a good feeder and finisher.

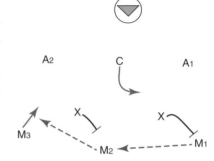

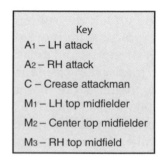

Key
A1 – LH attack
A2 – RH attack
C – Crease attackman
M1 – LH top midfielder
M2 – Center top midfielder
M3 – RH top midfield

**Figure 10.1** 3-3 vs. 2-3 zone.

The ball starts on top, and you get the ball to the top middleman as quickly as possible. When he has the ball and steps in to draw the defense, you can easily read what type of defense they're in. Three or four defensive sets are commonly used against the 3-3.

## Against 2-3 MDD

If your opponent is in a 2-3 zone, the two top defensemen attempt to play the three top offensive men while covering the three low offensive players man to man. In this set they are giving you the outside shot. Try to force one of the two top defenders to play the middleman, thereby giving one of your top men a free shot because he is momentarily uncovered. In this set, the middleman is the key to drawing the defensive player who is playing your best finisher. This creates the opportunity to set up an open shot for your best outside shooter (see figure 10.2).

## Against 2-1-2 MDD

The most popular defensive set against the 3-3, is the 2-1-2 string. In this set, the middle defensive player pops up from the creaseman to play the top middleman when he has the ball. The two low defensive men are supposed to bump up and squeeze the creaseman. The other two top wing defensive players are supposed to cut off the passing lanes to the low wing attackmen and yet still be in position to slide back to their man if they get the ball (see figure 10.3).

This defensive set has some weaknesses. The two top wing defensemen, particularly a short-stick midfielder, has a difficult time cutting off the passing lane to the low attackmen on his side. If the

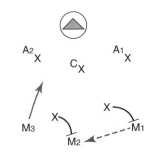

**Figure 10.2**   3-3 vs. 2-3 MDD.

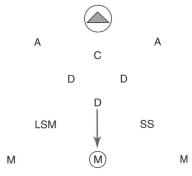

**Figure 10.3**   1-4-1 vs. 2-1-2 MDD.

defenseman playing the creaseman bumps up when the ball is on top, it makes it more difficult for the low wing defenseman to get back to his man.

Because you want to attack the splitter, target the center crease defender. For example, work the ball around from the top middle position, counterclockwise to the bottom left-handed attackman (A1). The A1 tries to find his primary option (creaseman), who bumped up high when the top left-handed player (M1) had the ball but has now come down to the onside pipe for the left-handed feed and right-handed shot. This puts a lot of pressure on the center defenseman, who is responsible for both the top right-handed player (M2) when the ball is any place on top and for the crease when the ball is in the wing spots. If the feed from the A1 is properly placed to the creaseman as he cuts to the ball, it makes it almost impossible for that center defenseman to make a legal check.

Sometimes the defense will overcompensate to cover the crease, thereby leaving someone else open. This is what is meant by reading the defense and immediately saying that one option is closed, so to go to the second or third option. This is also the beauty of an offense that teaches and encourages free choice to take what the defense gives you.

## Against a Box-and-One MDD

Another defensive set some teams use against the 3-3 set is the box and one. In this defense, one man, usually the short-stick midfielder, plays the crease man to man. The other four long-pole defensemen either play zone or a four-man rotation against the remaining five perimeter players. The key to beating the rotation of the defenseman is quick ball movement. It is difficult for the defenseman to defend against a quickly moving offense. See figure 10.4.

In a box-and-one zone defense, stay in a 3-3 for a while to see whether you can get a feed in the skip lanes from the top middle player (M2) to either the bottom left-handed attackman (A1) or the bottom right-handed attackman (A2). If not, continue your extra-man offense, which is a series of cuts from a 3-3-3 to a 1-3-2 into a 1-4-1.

From a 3-3 set, the top middle player (M2) passes to the top left-handed player (M1) who passes to the bottom left-handed attackman (A1). The A1 has rotated slightly higher and looks to M2 cutting onside (see figure 10.5a). If not open, A1 passes up top to M1 (see figure 10.5b). M1 checks inside for openings. If he finds none, M1 immediately passes back to A1 (see figure

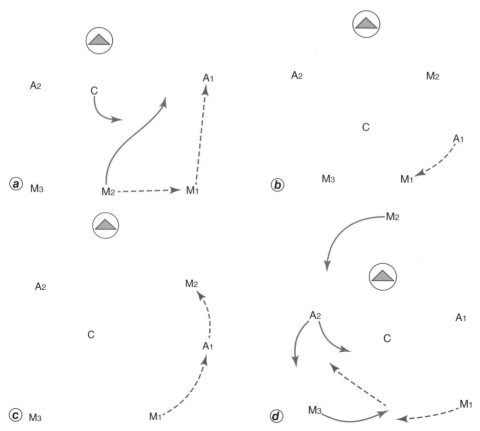

**Figure 10.4** 1-3-2 (L.I. play) vs. box-and-one MDD.

10.6) who looks inside. If there are no openings, A1 dumps the ball to M2, who is now at the goal line extended in an overload. If the defenseman stays with A1, then M2 (if open) can shoot. The only defensive slides to cover M2 are either the off-wing defenseman, leaving A1 possibly open, or the crease defenseman, leaving the creaseman open. If M2 has nothing on the overload, he passes the ball back to A1, who continues moving the ball clockwise around the perimeter. Meanwhile, M2 has rotated to X and is positioning himself to come around the cage for a sneak dodge or feed. The top right-handed player (M3) has rotated to the middle of the field where he got the ball from M1. He looks inside. If there are no openings, he passes the ball to the bottom right-handed player (A2), who has moved up into the area that M3 vacated. A2 is in a shooting position and has the option to shoot if open and if not, A2 looks to M2. M2 has the option to shoot if open or to feed M1, who is cutting down to the offside pipe. M2's other option is the creaseman on the offside. If no one is open, you have rotated from a 1-3-2 into a 1-4-1.

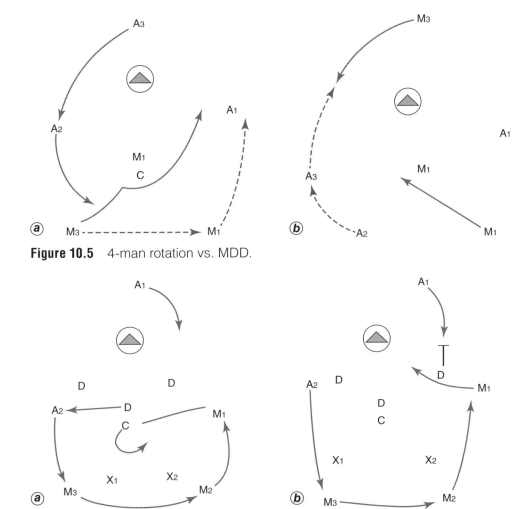

**Figure 10.5**   4-man rotation vs. MDD.

**Figure 10.6**   Continuing the 4-man rotation to create an open shot.

# 1-4-1 EMO

Once you are in a 1-4-1, continue to look inside to either creaseman. You are in a freelance scheme for the remainder of the EMO. Only three men will handle the ball in this formation: the man at X or either wingman. The two creasemen and the top midfielders are primary shooters. The two creasemen do not necessarily pick for each other but must move into the vacated space created by the shifting defensemen. They move from high to low or low to high, depending on the position of the ball. When the wingmen have the ball, the onside creaseman shifts low and the offside creaseman moves high. When the ball is at X, they both start high to give themselves room to cut to the ball. The offside creaseman can either cut low for the cross-cage feed or pop onside high to overload. The feeder at X must penetrate the defense to force a slide, see whether there's an opening, or pass the ball quickly to the onside wingmen. The wingmen options are the same: Penetrate and force a slide if possible, see whether there's an opening, and if not, pass quickly to X. When the wingmen have the ball, the creasemen must position themselves in a high–low set. The onside creaseman is low and the offside creaseman goes high. All three feeders have the same options. As long as they penetrate and draw a slide, they have four defensemen playing five offensive players. The key is to move the ball quickly, force the defense to slide, and then find the open man. This forces your offensive players to learn how to read defenses and to adjust accordingly. If you have a set play and the opponent has scouted your players, you may not be able to adjust quickly. You can use set plays on EMO, but when you are accustomed to freelancing, you can go to your other options if you don't get the shot you want.

# 1-3-2 EMO: LONG ISLAND

A shorter version of the regular 3-3 play is from a 1-3-2 set. The Long Island play is the same as the 3-3 play, except that it begins from the diagonal cut from the top right-handed player (M3) when the bottom left-handed attackman (A1) gets the ball (see figure 10.5a). Eliminate the overload look and go right into the diagonal sneak into a 1-4-1. This play is useful for several reasons. Sometimes with the regular 3-3 play, you don't get to complete all of the options. Try to use this play at least once before halftime to give the coaches and players an opportunity to see how your opponent defends it. This play gives you a much quicker look at the sneak from behind and the diagonal cut by the far-side top midfielder. If the creaseman is covered by the far wing defenseman, look to feed the attackman on the wing. These are the preferred shots from a 1-3-2 set. They are called layups and are difficult for goalies to defend. After the top left-handed player (M1) makes his cut, stay in your 1-4-1. Because this play develops quickly, you can use this for 30-second penalties (see figure 10.5b).

# 1-3-2 EMO

This second series for your extra-man offense can be part of your regular zone offense against a six-man zone. When the ball is on top, use the carry-and-throwback series, in which a rotation of four players maintain the same spacing. When the ball is behind, use the wing-drive box rotation. For example, the top right-handed player (M3) has possession of the ball in this set. The top middle player (M2) rotates away from the M3 as the M3 comes his way. This is called stretching. All four perimeter players rotate in the same direction as the ball carrier. As the M3 carries the ball across the top, he looks to the following players as they enter the seams of the zone (where both zones meet). His options are 1) the M2 stretching away from him, 2) the top left-handed player (M1) crossing the face of the goal, or 3) the creaseman curling into the soft spot of the zone. If none of these options are open, M3 rolls to the outside and throws back to the bottom right-handed attackman (A2), who has rotated into the area that he vacated. After he passes to A2, he stretches away down the lane as the ball is carried toward him.

When the ball is at X, use a four-man rotation called wing drives. Initiate the wing-drive cut as the ball carrier drives the goal line extended (GLE). As the wingman makes his cut, the top midfielder cuts down to the area he vacated (the drive). All four perimeter men continue to rotate at the same time. This offense is particularly effective against man-down units that only pick up at the GLE. The ball carrier has a simple read because there will be a 4v3 overload on the ball side. See figures 5.2 and 5.3 on pages 72 and 73 for diagrams. The ball carrier simply has to read who slides to pick him up at the GLE:

1. If it's the defender who is playing the crease and the far top defender slid to cover the crease, the ball carrier should still be able to get the shot off. When a defender is behind the creaseman, the creaseman shields his stick with his body as he steps to the ball. If the offside defender slides to cover the crease, the wing attackman (A2) should be open.

2. If it's the onside wing defenseman who picks up the ball carrier at the GLE, several options are available. The first is to initiate the wing-drive rotation. This forces (M2) to make a decision. If he rotates to cover the top right-handed player (M1) on the wing drive (cut from the wing to the onside pipe), the top middle player (M2) will be open on the drive (cut down the lane). If he (X2) doesn't rotate down, M1 will be open for a shot right at the face of the goal (layup). The wing-drive rotation continues giving the attackman at the goal line extended (A2) multiple looks on the ball side. The creaseman, when being played man to man simply takes his man high and to the offside pipe, giving the wing (M1) and the drive (M2) players more space. Remember, all four perimeter players continually rotate.

When the creaseman is played man to man, a second option opens up in this series. When the top cutter, who is driving, is left-handed, you don't want him taking a left-handed shot on the drive cut. In this situation, the wing cutter (A2) picks the crease defender. The creaseman is your primary option. The timing and spacing on these cuts can vary from the traditional cutting game. This must be part of your regular rotation so that your timing and spacing is coordinated.

The way your extra-man offense attacks your opponent's man-down defense depends on how they attempt to defend your formation. The following summarizes your options.

## 3-3 Offensive Set

1. **Against a 2-3 zone**: In this zone, your opponent plays the three low offensive players man to man and attempts to play the top three shooters with two men. Against this set, set up your best outside shooter. For example, if the top right-handed player (M3) is your best outside shooter, get the ball to the top left-handed player (M1). The M1 draws and dumps to the top middle player (M2), who draws the defender, splitting him and the M3, and then dumps it to the M3 for the time-and-room shot. See figure 10.2 for an example.

2. **Against a 2-1-2 string**: In this defense, the center defender is responsible for two men, who are usually set up in a line with each other, hence the term string. In this set, the middle defenseman plays the top middle player (M2) when the ball is up top. When the ball is down to either low attackman, he is responsible for the low center creaseman. You want to skip the ball to the lower wingmen if the lanes are open or get the ball to one of the lower wingmen to feed the creaseman onside. The low attackman (A2 or A1) can either shoot, feed the crease, or feed the opposite wing. If those inside lanes are not open to the low attackman, M2 can pass to either the top right-handed or left-handed player. Either of these players can then pass to their onside wingman, who has the same options as described earlier—crease, cutter, back pipe. See figure 10.3 for an example.

3. **Against a box and one**: You want to stretch, carry, or throw back. Stretch means to rotate away from the ball carrier, maintaining the same spacing on the perimeter as he carries the ball toward you. Throw back means to pass the ball back to the man rotating into the area that you just vacated. The player carrying the ball might have to roll to the outside and throw back if he's being guarded closely. See figure 10.6 for an example.

When the ball is behind, draw the defender at the GLE and overload the ball side with the low wing (M1) cutting back door and the top midfielder cutting to the ball into the vacated area. This rotation is continuous. Spacing and timing are crucial so that the men on the far side of the rotation have backup responsibilities as well as providing opportunities to shoot. For example, the top right-handed player (M3) backs up the top middle's (M2) cut. The creaseman backs up the M2's cut. See figure 10.6 for an example.

When the ball is on top, M3 carries the ball across the top and reads his options. Option 1 is M2 as he stretches down the lane. Option 2 is M1 going back door as he cuts across the cage. Option 3 is the bottom right-hand attackman (A2) in the skip lane. And option 4 is the creaseman on a pop-out. If none of these options are open, roll and throw back to the creaseman when he gets to the far side of the cage.

## 1-3-2 Offensive Set

Get the ball to X and try to sneak. A sneak occurs when the player at X cuts to the GLE when the ball is on top. Feed the crease, diagonal cut or offside wing. A diagonal cut is when the far-side player cuts across the face of the goal to receive a feed for a shot. The ball starts on top with (M2). M2 passes to M1. When M1 passes down the side to A1, M2 cuts down on side as an option. C curls behind M2's cut as another option. If neither option is open, A1 reverses the ball back to M1, who rotates it to M3. If neither option is open, M2 rotates to X. M3 passes to A3. A1 passes to M1, who sneaks from the GLE. M1's options are first to shoot, second to feed the onside cutter (M1), third to feed the offside creaseman (C), or fourth to feed cross cage to A1.

## 1-3-2 Offensive Set vs. Box and One

When playing against zone with no pressure behind, the defense will pick up at the GLE when the ball is behind the cage. You use the 4- or 5-man rotation.

The first set is a wing-drive rotation. When the wing defenseman picks up the ball at the GLE, slide the wing attackman (BL) behind him to the onside pipe. At the same time, the top midfielder cuts down the lane into the area vacated by BL. This is a continuous rotation with all four perimeter players rotating from one spot to another.

## Extra Man vs. Two Men Down

You can use two plays against two men down. The first is the Long Island play. The second is the 1-4-1 rotate. On this play, the four perimeter players use the carry throwback technique, looking for the player who gave them the ball as they stretch away into the seam. The other options are the two creasemen who are playing high and low inside. For example, when the top right-handed player (A1) carries from X to the wing, his options are the creaseman and top left-handed player (M3) inside and the bottom right-handed attackman (A2) rotating away (stretching). If no one is open, he rolls and throws back to the bottom left-handed attackman (A2) at X. The options are the same for all four players on the perimeters: crease, stretch, or throw.

# EMO SETS VS. MAN-DOWN DENY

Extra-man offense requires specific preparation when defenses use a variety of deny and shutoff techniques. When an EMO team has a dominant player, this is most likely to occur. Recognition early in the penalty is crucial to avoiding wasting precious time reorganizing the set or play.

## Deny Player at X

Rotate the player being shut off to the crease and use the Long Island play.

## Deny Area X

Use your carry, stretch, and throwback plays previously mentioned in extra-man offense. These include a variety of options when the defense attempts to deny the ball at X.

Emphasize the importance of patience, shot selection, and a high lacrosse IQ for your extra-man offense. Extra-man offense provides an opportunity to put your best six offensive players on the field against a man-down defense for the duration of the penalty time. The skills of the offensive players should be highlighted in the preparation of sets. Rely on players' instincts to recognize potential scoring opportunities. Encourage players to read the defense and take what is given.

# CHAPTER 11

# Man-Down Defense

As mentioned in chapter 10, man-down defense (MDD) occurs when a team is penalized with a time-serving foul ranging from 30 to 60 seconds. At the discretion of the official, personal fouls can be extended to 3 minutes. To teach your team how to play MDD, continue the transition defense principles in which a team plays shorthanded. Effective coaching requires a simulation of a game situation in which 5 seconds are added to allow the player time to re-enter the field of play and re-create the 6v6 half-field matchup. Success in MDD relies on giving up low-percentage shots from the outside. Do not give up high-percentage layups inside.

The following description outlines your defensive philosophy in playing 5v6 against most formations. The man playing the ball pressures the ball inside the offensive zone. The two adjacent players are responsible first for the man in their area, second for the passing lane to the second man around away from the ball, and last to back up the ball if the defender is dodged. The two defenders farthest from the ball play a zone against the other three players. If one of these three players is playing the crease, then the farthest man plays him and the other man splits the remaining two players. It is essential that those two defenders be responsible for the adjacent players to the ball and must cut off the passing lanes to the next man around (skip lanes). This allows the two players who are playing three men to drop in and to help out on the crease. The man playing the creaseman plays a slightly different technique than you use in regular 6v6 man-to-man defense. For example, when the ball is at X, the farthest top-side defender drops into the crease. In this case, however, instead of playing between the ball and the creaseman, he plays behind the creaseman on the stick side. The other lone top-side defender splits the two remaining offensive players.

The following are plays against standard offensive formations. Each includes a figure showing the position of the offensive players in strategic locations on their half of the field. They are numbered from behind the cage moving out to the restraining line.

# AGAINST 1-3-2

Players are labeled a follows: crease defenseman (C), two wing defensemen (W), top long-stick midfielder (LSM), and the remaining short-stick defender (SS). During the drill, the defender labeled as the crease defender plays X when the ball is behind and crease when the ball is on top. The two wing defensemen play the wings. The LSM and short-stick midfielder start out playing up top when the ball is there and the player away from the ball slides to the crease when the ball goes to

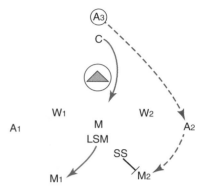

**Figure 11.1** MDD vs. 1-3-2.

X (see figure 11.1). When the ball is at X, the positions are as follows. The crease defenseman pressures the ball at X. W1 and W2 have two responsibilities: First, they are responsible for the man in their zone, and second, they must cut off the passing lanes to the man on top. For example, W1 is responsible for the passing lane to M1. W2 on the other side has the same two responsibilities, except he is responsible for the passing lane to M2. SS started inside, so his responsibility is the creaseman. For drill purposes, SS guards the creaseman from behind. The LSM splits M1 and M2.

When the ball is passed to A2 on the wing, responsibilities are as follows. W2 must get to A2 as the ball gets there. The crease defenseman releases to onside the goal line extended (GLE) and is responsible for the low passing lane from A2 to A1. LSM slides over to pick up M2 and is responsible for the passing lane to M1. The two men farthest from the ball are responsible for covering the crease area. W1 slides over and plays the creaseman if he's down low. He helps out on the crease and must be aware of the high passing lane from A2 to A1. The short-stick midfielder also helps out on the crease. If the creaseman pops high, the short-stick midfielder covers him. If the creaseman stays low, the off-wing defenseman (W1) has him. Meanwhile, the crease defenseman positioned at the GLE has his stick in the passing lane as well.

> When the ball is on the wing, three men help out to cover the creaseman. This can only be accomplished if all three are vigilant in the passing lanes.

When the ball gets passed up top to M2, SS picks him up. W2 drops off and is in the passing lane from M2 to A3 should he attempt to sneak to the ball side. LSM is responsible for M1, but he has a stick in the passing lane from M2 to A1. The rule for all adjacent defenders is to have their stick in the lane and their body toward the man in their zone. In short, it's stick in, body out. As the ball moves from M2 to M1, everyone adjusts accordingly. The rules here are the same for both adjacent defenders (W1 and LSM), but note how the off-wing defenseman and crease defensemen slough in (or form into a help position) to cover the crease area. If the offensive creaseman is ball side, the crease defenseman has primary responsibility. W2 helps out on the crease if he moves offside. Note how the two farthest defensive players (C and W2) are responsible for the three men farthest from the ball. This can only be accomplished if the two adjacent defenders (W1 and LSM) cut off the passing lanes inside. For example, LSM must cut the passing lanes off from A2. W1 must cutoff the onside sneak lane to A3. The same fundamentals are emphasized against all offensive sets.

## AGAINST 2-1-3

In an offensive set that has two men behind, the wingmen are responsible for the attackmen behind the cage. If the formation has an odd set on top (e. g., 2-1-3, 2-3-1, or 1-4-1), the crease defenseman picks up the lone or center offensive player when the ball is on top. The responsibilities of all the players are the same as earlier stated. The man playing the ball carrier presses the ball. Two adjacent defenders play the man in their zone and cut off the passing lanes. The two men farthest from the ball and the crease defenseman

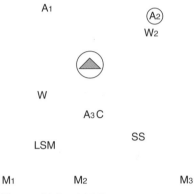

**Figure 11.2** MDD vs. 2-1-3.

are played by the two remaining defenders (see figure 11.2). If A2 has the ball behind, W2 plays the ball, and W1 is responsible for A1 but is still be in the passing lanes from W2 to M1. The short-stick midfielder on top is responsible for M3 and the passing lane from W2 to M2. The crease defenseman plays A3 as shown. LSM, the man farthest from the ball, splits the two men farthest from the ball (M1 and M2). As the ball is passed up top to M3, the following slides occur. The crease defenseman is responsible for the middle top offensive player (M2). W1 and W2 move up to the crease area as shown. W1 has primary responsibility for A3, as long as he stays low or to the offside. If he pops out high, the crease defenseman helps. W2 helps by putting his stick in the passing lane and picks up A3 if he overloads ball side. As the ball moves to center top, the crease defenseman comes out and plays him. The short stick and LSM drop off into the passing lanes and remain aware of the creaseman (A3) if he pops out high into their zones.

Note how the defensive concepts are always the same. The adjacent men slough in to cover lanes; the two men farthest from the ball are responsible for the remaining three offensive players. The farthest defensive player sloughs into the crease, leaving the farthest offensive player uncovered away from the ball. In most situations, two or more players are responsible for helping on the crease. As the ball moves around the perimeter, it is essential that the men move on and off the ball quickly and constantly swivel their head back and forth so they are aware of the man whose passing lane they are responsible for. This fundamental was emphasized earlier in chapter 3 in a 3v2 drill and 6v5 drill.

## AGAINST 2-3-1

The responsibilities are the same as in a 2-1-3. The wing defensemen play the ball behind. The crease defenseman is responsible for the crease and the midfielder on top. LSM and short-stick midfielders start out playing the wing midfielders (see figure 11.3).

Use the 2-3-1 set when the offensive team has a strong shooter who can be placed at the top of the set. Placement of the five other offensive players in the area closest to the goal forces the defense to concentrate their efforts on defending that area. This will create scoring opportunities for the shooter.

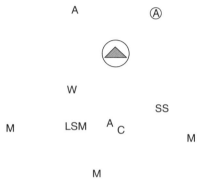

**Figure 11.3**    MDD vs. 2-3-1.

## AGAINST 2-2-2

Against this set, the responsibilities of the wing defensemen and the top defenders (LSM and SS) are the same as the 2-3-1. The crease defenseman plays the onside crease when the ball is behind and favors the ball-side creaseman when the ball is out front. The short stick and LSM responsibilities are the same as in other sets. The far-side top defender drops in and helps on the crease when the ball is behind (see figure 11.4). Against this set, pressure the ball hard forcing it to the inside when the ball is on top. Try to force a dodge from the top because you have an extra defender, the crease defender (C), to back up the ball. You can use a fire call to block off an adjacent pass so that you can double the ball.

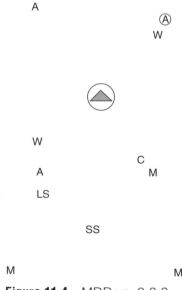

**Figure 11.4**    MDD vs. 2-2-2.

# AGAINST CIRCLE

Against this formation follow all the basic defensive rules. The man playing the ball pressures the ball. The two adjacent players are responsible for the man in their zone and must cutoff the passing lanes. The two defensive players farthest from the ball split the three offensive players. Defensive players follow a cutter through the crease and stick with him if he stays on the crease or pick him up on the perimeter if he cuts through the crease. If this happens, continue to adjust by following your defensive rules. The two men adjacent to the ball have the same responsibilities as stated earlier; the two men farthest from the ball adjust to their offensive player. (See figure 11.5*a*). You may use a fire call against this set. For example, when the ball is in the top middle and your opponent has two or more players below the GLE, you momentarily have them outnumbered 5v4 on top. If you feel you have a favorable matchup on your LSM, use your fire call (see figure 11.5*b*).

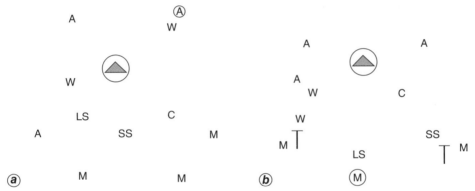

**Figure 11.5**   MDD vs. *(a)* circle and *(b)* fire call.

# AGAINST 3-3

When the ball is in the top middle, it is essential that the adjacent men (LSM and SS) cut off the skip lanes to A1 and A2 (see figure 11.6). W1 and W2 must pinch in on A3 to prevent an easy layup. When the ball gets to the top wing midfielder, the crease defenseman (C) must drop down and play the top ball-side of creaseman (A3). The far-side wingman (W1) must play the backside of creaseman A3. The onside wingman (W2) splits between A2 and A3. If wing attack-

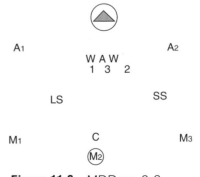

**Figure 11.6**   MDD vs. 3-3.

man (A2) gets the ball, he must be pressured by the wing (W2). Defender C must cover the crease attackman (A3) on ball side. The off-wing defenseman must be in the lane between A2 and A1 and help if A3 cuts low. The onside short stick must be in the lane between A2 and M2. The short-stick midfielder must discourage that pass and influence them to pass it back up to M3. This allows time for him to make the slide to M3 and allows time for defender C to slide up and cover M2.

## AGAINST AUSSIE

Against this set, play the same techniques as you do against the 3-3 set. Emphasize taking away the three layups and all three attackmen, and, if necessary, give them the outside shot, preferably from M2. When the top center midfielder (M2) has the ball, the center defenseman (C) slides up and plays him (see figure 11.7). LSM and the short stick again cutoff the lanes to A1 and A2 respectively. The two low defensemen (W1 and W2) pinch in on the center attackman A3. When the top wing midfielder (M3) gets the ball, he is picked

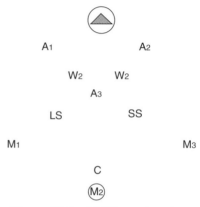

**Figure 11.7** MDD vs. Aussie.

up by the short-stick midfielder. The far-side wingman slides up to cover the creaseman (A3) from the backside. The center defenseman (C) drops to cover the lane from M3 to M1. LSM drops in to help on the creaseman (A3). If A2 gets the ball, the wing defenseman (W2) pressures him hard to prevent a shot or easy pass to either A1 or A3. Defenseman C and LSM both slough down to help on A3. The principles of this defensive scheme are the same concepts. The two men farthest from the ball cover the crease. The two adjacent men cover the man in their zone and inside lanes. This is the same concept whether the ball is in the top wing or in the lower wings.

## AGAINST 1-4-1

Against 1-4-1, you must make an important adjustment. Because the best outside shooters are normally the man on top and the wing perimeter players (A1 and A2), you want your long poles playing these positions whenever possible. The short stick plays inside on the crease. For example, when M1 has the ball on top, LSM plays that position (see figure 11.8). The reason for this is twofold. M1, the top midfielder, is

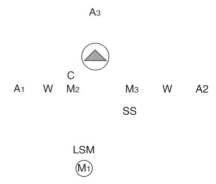

**Figure 11.8** MDD vs. 1-4-1.

usually your opponent's top shooter, and you need a long pole in the lane when either wingmen (A1 or A2) have the ball. In a 1-4-1 offense, quite often the wingmen step out high and attempt to pass wing to wing. For example, A1 looks to skip the ball across to A2. It would be difficult for a short stick to cut off that passing lane. When A1 has the ball, the crease defender has the low skip lane across the face of the cage, and LSM has the skip lane in the high lane previously mentioned. The low skip lane is passed to the off crease (M3) if he's low or the far lane (A2). The LSM skip lane would be to the off crease (M3) if he pops high or the far wing (A2). To accomplish this, both long poles (crease and LSM) must keep their sticks to the inside passing lanes and swivel their heads to watch the far-side players. Anytime a wingman has the ball, the short-stick midfielder plays the onside crease and the offside wingman sloughs in to play the offside crease.

When the ball is at X, the crease defender pressures the ball. The LSM drops down and plays the offside midfielder from behind. The two wingmen play in the lanes covering their wingman but are helping in the lanes to the top man (M1) if he should rotate to their side. When the ball is on top, you have a defensive 1-4 look. However, when the ball is in the wings, the defensive formation is a 1-3-1 look. When A2 has the ball on the wing, the positions are as follows: The short stick slides over to the onside crease. The far wing plays the offside crease. LSM drops down, covering the skip lane from A2 to A1. The crease defender comes to the GLE to cover the stick lane to the offside crease or offside wing, should they drop low. This is the basic defense against 1-4-1.

## FIRE CALL

Depending on your matchups against a 1-4-1 set, if you feel that one of your long poles has a decisive advantage over the player he is guarding, you might initiate this adjustment to the defense. In the fire call, the two men adjacent to the ball deny the pass to their man, and the player playing the ball pressures the ball and attempts to either take it away or force a bad pass. This call may be by position only. For example, if the player at X (A3) has the ball, the crease defender pressures him while the wingmen deny the ball to A1 and A2 respectively. The same scenario could be used on top when M1 has the ball. You can use this call in regular team defense as well. In a man-down situation, it can be effective because most offenses do not expect it and might be caught off guard. Use this only when you feel that your long pole has a decisive advantage over the man he is guarding.

## MAN-DOWN PRINCIPLES

Man-down defense is a critical component of your overall defensive philosophy, and you teach it the same as the basic defensive strategies. Similar to the power play in hockey, this is the equivalent of playing shorthanded for a predetermined amount of time. Teach your players that the best man-down defense is to avoid committing penalties. However, it is reasonable, based on the physical nature of the sport, that penalty situations will occur.

1. Keep sticks to the inside to cut off passing lanes, do not allow skip passes, and force perimeter passes that do not create scoring opportunities.

2. Always step toward the inside on a perimeter rotation slide to prevent the offense from splitting the seam with a skip pass.

3. Be slow to go when the ball is behind; make sure coverage is available on the slide man's player. Be quicker to go with a pass from behind to up top. The defender must breakdown as he approaches the offensive player to avoid lunging and being vulnerable to a quick dodge.

4. Play high on the wing when the ball is behind, force cuts underneath, and be ready to squeeze the wing shooter by checking through the hands to prevent the follow-through.

5. Position yourself in a man–you–ball defensive triangle to create a defensive presence and be prepared to slide, step to the ball, or deny the passing lane.

## MAN-DOWN DEFENSE SITUATIONS AS PART OF THE PRACTICE SCHEDULE

1. Incorporate extra-man offense against man-down defense during practice while other team members work on specific skills, settled offense, half-field transition drills, and individual skill drills.

2. Incorporate short periods of EMO vs. MDD during breaks between teaching and practicing specific concepts, for example in the time between positional skill sessions for attack vs. defense or half-field 6v6.

3. Before going full field, go live EMO vs. MDD and set specific goals.

4. Time EMO vs. MDD sessions to simulate game situations. The simulation allows the offense to play through the 6v5 to 6v6 half-field offense and the defense to communicate from MDD to an all-even situation by returning to matchups with individual players.

5. Identify and develop a scout team to simulate the opponent's EMO and MDD units. This team is made up of players who will work to create realistic looks throughout the season.

6. Work with multiple backup players at all positions on EMO and MDD.

7. Create a competitive atmosphere when going live in practice. Set specific percentages and goals to be met during challenge matches.

8. Teach and review all game situations related to EMO and MDD. This includes face-offs, clears, rides, substitution patterns, short time, and multiple-player sets, such as two men up, two men down, and other configurations.

9. Work EMO and MDD into the normal flow of practice to simulate the game situations that will occur. Similar to coaching special teams in football, it is suggested that 15 percent of practice time should be devoted to this important part of the game. Just as basketball players practice free throws when they are tired, lacrosse players should work on EMO and MDD when they are physically and mentally fatigued to create a more realistic gamelike experience.

# MAN DOWN USING DENY AND CUT-OFF TECHNIQUES DRILL

## Purpose

Neutralize an opponent with a dominant player.

## Setup

The setup depends on the location of the dominant player.

Your deny call is red plus the number of the player you want to cutoff. For example, if their playmaker is number 15 and is playing at X, the call is red 15. If their best shooter is on the crease and his number is 10, the call is red 10. When you cut off a player, put your best short-stick defender on him. This way, you still have your four long poles playing the remaining five players.

## Pro

This creates a different look that forces the offensive team to make adjustments.

## Con

Playing 6v5 is more of an advantage for the defense, compared to playing 5v4.

## MAN-DOWN DENY AT CREASE VS. 1-3-2 DRILL

### Purpose

Keep the primary shooter from receiving the ball directly in front of the cage.

### Setup

To deny the crease player, play 4v5 on the perimeter.

The four perimeter defensemen play the same technique they play in the zone defense as well as in the 6v5 drill. The man playing the ball pressures the ball, and the two adjacent men play the man in their zone and are responsible for the skip lane to the next adjacent player. The man farthest from the ball splits two players.

### Pro

This forces less-talented shooters to handle the ball.

### Con

Perimeter shooters will have more space to create scoring opportunities.

## MAN-DOWN DENY AT X VS. 1-3-2 DRILL

### Purpose

Deny the feeder at X (the area directly behind the cage).

### Setup

Deny the feeder in the prime location for assists.

In this formation, although you are playing the same technique as earlier outlined in man down defense principles, it puts a lot more pressure on the man farthest from the ball. The man farthest from the ball usually splits two players, but in this situation, one is the crease defender. It is important that the adjacent players deny the skip lanes and encourage perimeter passing.

### Pro

It forces less-talented players to distribute the ball.

### Con

It forces the defense to play 4v5 above the goal line extended.

# MAN-DOWN DENY AT X VS. 1-4-1 DRILL

## Purpose

Deny the feeder at X (the area directly behind the cage).

## Setup

Deny the feeder in a prime location for assists.

When denying X against 1-4-1, the responsibilities of the adjacent players change. There is no skip lane to defend but there is potential for a far more dangerous feed to the onside crease defender. When the ball is on either wing, the onside wingman pressures the ball from the top side, preventing his man from going high. The defender playing the top man cuts off the skip to the far wing and the offside wingman playing the crease is responsible for the low skip lane, wing to wing.

## Pro

This forces less-talented players to distribute the ball.

## Con

This forces the defense to play 4v5 above the goal line extended.

# MAN-DOWN DENY UP TOP VS. 1-4-1 DRILL

## Purpose

Deny your opponent's best shooter.

## Setup

Deny up top and play 4v5 below.

   The responsibilities of the defense are somewhat similar to the man-down deny of X. For example, when the ball is at X, the three defenders split the four players along the face of the cage. The two outside wingmen help on the passing lanes to the creaseman on their side. When the ball is on the wing, the crease defender comes above the ball side GLE and helps on the low skip lane from one wing to the other. The offside wingman is responsible for the offside creaseman and also for the high lane from wing to wing.

## Pro

It takes away the best offensive scorer's shooting spot.

## Con

You must defend 5v4 with your remaining players.

# MAN-DOWN DENY OF WINGS VS. 1-4-1 DRILL

## Purpose

Deny a shooter with a dominant hand.

## Setup

Identify which wing would be most vulnerable based on right- and left-hand ability.

In this formation, when the ball is at X, the defensive man who is responsible for the top man comes down and plays the creaseman on the side of the strong hand of the top shooter. For example, if he is a strong left-handed shooter and the ball is at X, the defenseman plays behind the creaseman. When the ball is up top, the crease defender plays the offside crease defender. When the ball is on the wing, the crease defender again plays the onside crease, and the top defender drops down and helps in the high lane should either crease defender pop high.

## Pro

It denies the dangerous wing shot.

## Con

It creates openings on passes to the opposite wing.

# TWO MEN DOWN VS. 1-3-2 DRILL

## Purpose

Concede a low-percentage shot.

## Setup

Create a tight box with four defensive players.

When you are two men down, play the same technique as on a 6v6 zone or 6v5 man down. For example, you still pressure the ball carrier. The two adjacent men have the same responsibilities: They play the man in their zone and cutoff the passing lanes to the adjacent players. The man farthest from the ball sloughs down to help on the crease. The man farthest from the ball sloughs down into the crease. When the ball is on the wing, the wingman pressures the ball, the defender who is playing X helps on the low crease, the far defender sloughs into the crease, and the adjacent player on top cuts off the lane to the second man from the ball. These rules put you in a diamond formation whenever the ball is above the GLE.

## Pro

Perimeter passes use up penalty time.

## Con

This is difficult to accomplish against quick ball movement.

## Variation: Two Men Down vs. 1-4-1

When the ball is up on top, the four long poles play the same techniques described earlier against the man-down deny X against 1-4-1. They play the same technique when the ball is at X. When the ball is on the wings, the onside wingman pressures the ball, the two adjacent defenders slough into the crease and cutoff the inside lanes, and the far wingman splits the two creasemen, favoring the onside man. The man-down team, when down two men against 1-4-4, plays a 1-3 anytime the ball is on the perimeter.

## Variation: Two Men Down vs. 3-3

When playing two men down against 3-3, follow the same rules as previously mentioned in man down defense principles. Emphasize that the man farthest from the ball slides down and helps on the crease.

## Variation: Two Men Down vs. Aussie

Although the rules are nearly the same, you will make one important adjustment. The man adjacent to the ball, who is playing a low wingman, gives up his lane responsibility to guard his man more tightly. For example, if the opposite wingman has the ball, he must cut off his man. The man farthest from the ball has crease responsibilities.

## Variation: Two Men Down vs. 2-2-2

This is one of the few times you make an exception to the rule in man down that you do not pressure the ball behind the cage. When you pick the opponent up at the GLE, you have reduced their advantage from 6v4 to at most 5v4. When the ball is up top, the onside man pressures the ball. The two low defenders play behind their creaseman and are responsible for the lane to the attackman behind the cage. The adjacent top midfielder sloughs in to help in the lane to the offside creaseman. When the ball goes behind, the onside defenseman picks up at the GLE, the offside defenseman slides over to the onside creaseman, and the far-side midfielder drops down to the offside crease. After the ball is passed over to the other attackman behind, the low defenders slide to ball side and have onside responsibilities to pick up the ball at the GLE, and the offside defenseman has the onside crease. The far top-side defender slides in and plays the offside crease, and the top-side defender has his man and is responsible for the skip lane.

The philosophy and strategies for man-down defense emphasize the importance of the same sound defensive principles that highlight your transition defense. The most effective teaching tool is to reinforce the principles you established when defending fast breaks, slow breaks, and transition offense. Any time the offense has a numbers advantage, the defense must play to force perimeter passing and a low-percentage shot. These man-down situations are time specific, based on the duration of the penalty.

# CHAPTER 12

# Special Situations

This chapter identifies a variety of special situations that occur during lacrosse games. Recognizing them and playing them appropriately are important for the success of your lacrosse program. Included in the special situations are the key elements of goalie play and face-off techniques.

## GOALTENDING

The goalie position is pivotal to success in lacrosse. The ability to stop shots by making saves, to lead the defense, and to communicate to teammates will contribute to successful goalie play.

### Teaching Fundamentals

A strong execution of the fundamentals of goalie play are crucial for success in this vital position. Work on basic skills at the beginning of practice. These skills include body and stick positioning, proper footwork, and lower- and upper-body movement. Many coaches work with the goalie without using the goalie stick to emphasize fundamentals.

Instructions to the goalie should be clear and concise. Keep it simple, focus on fundamentals and good habits, and be active in the prepractice warm up, which is an important teaching time in each session. Spend a minimum of 15 minutes with each goalie if possible. Introduce proper techniques, reinforce prior learning, and provide feedback.

The first area for instruction is proper positioning in the crease area and between the pipes. Foot positioning should be balanced and set to anticipate every shot. The crease is the area encircling the cage occupied by the goalie. Always step to the ball first with the ball-side foot. The lower-body movement creates the upper-body and stick movement that follow. Constantly reinforce stepping to the ball. Hands should be placed so that the top hand is near the throat of the stick and the lower hand grasps the area near the bottom end of the stick. Always keep the stick in front of your body and be ready to react to ball movement from a pass, feed, or shot. The head of the stick should move through the ball when attempting to make the save. Your head should be on every pass, feed, or shot to create the movement of seeing the ball into your stick. This is important on both high and low shots.

Begin with a discussion of proper foot positioning: Be set and balanced for the shot, move into each shot by playing the ball aggressively, step to the ball, be in the path, and stay and move through the ball. It is important to know where you are in relation to the crease area and the goal. Use the pipes of the cage as a reminder of where you are as you move to the ball location. The semicircle (3 feet from the front in relation to the pipes) allows you to move to the ball location. The cage is always stationary, allowing you a constant reminder of your position and the proper angles to play.

After setting the position of the lower body by balancing your weight heel to toe, keeping your head up and back straight, you should move on to proper hand location by placing your top hand near the throat and your bottom hand near the butt end of the stick.

Check stick and hand position before each shot and maintain it into and through the shot. Keep your stick head facing the shooter, with the top hand at the head. Your hands and stick should be out in front of your body and move through a full range of motion.

The next area to address is your head. Stay on every shot, and the body will follow the head: Stay behind, beside, or over the ball. Do not let the ball play you, and always be aggressive toward the shot. Play the ball in front, and step to the ball moving your feet and body into the path of the ball. Keep proper positioning at all times. Be set, hold position, and react on the release of the ball.

### Keys to Proper Technique

These are the three key areas for beginning players to concentrate on: Step with the foot to ball side and use the correct foot to the correct side, keep the stick out in front at the proper height and the head flat to the shooter, and always move the feet forward to the shot location

## Blocking Passes to Deny Scoring Opportunities

The goalie can help reduce the number of shots that will reach the cage. By maintaining proper body and stick position, he can block feeds from behind and across the cage. Properly turning by pivoting the head first so it turns faster than the body and pivoting hard on the inside foot, the goalie can anticipate the feed and ball location and stop the shot.

## Controlling the Crease Area

The crease area protects the goalie and his domain. Communication to defensive players when the ball is on the ground or in the crease area can prevent a potential scoring opportunity. The goalie must aggressively play all loose balls and unsettled action around the crease area.

Teach this by reviewing the proper techniques for a check-sticks call, which instructs all defensive players to check their opponent's stick or to body-check by screening and giving the goalie a clear path to pick up the ball. The 7v6 advantage in favor of the defense should allow control and possession of the loose ball by the goalie.

## Outlet Passes

The ability to clear the ball quickly after a save or defensive possession provides a dangerous offensive weapon. This is accomplished by gaining control of the ball. On making a save, the goalie should immediately look up the field to the wing areas or to the defensive corner of the field. The goalie uses the allotted 4 seconds of crease time to survey the situation and let the play develop. He moves within the crease area with possession to create a clear field of vision and create a favorable position for the pass. He does not force the ball into a crowded area, which could result in a turnover. He wants to put the right touch on each pass, avoid throwing too long or too short, and use practice time for outlet passes. If no safe outlet pass is available, the goalie should move behind and out of the crease area to restart the play.

## Communication

Skillful communication must be mastered to attain success in the goalie position. Goalies should be constant and consistent in all calls, practice communication as a positional skill, speak loudly and clearly with authority, be specific and precise, and always be positive and constructive. Key points to communicate include ball location, matchup, backup, and potential and defensive slide. Goalies call check on feeds and passes and must be able to initiate clearing patterns.

## GENERAL WARM-UP DRILL

### Purpose
Create an awareness of positioning and build confidence.

### Setup
The initial warm-up drills can be done with the goalie in the crease area playing without a stick.

### Execution
The coach throws a rubber ball or tennis ball by hand to various locations.

### Coaching Points
Remind the goalie to step to the ball. The upper body follows lower body. Tell the goalie, Play the ball. Do not let the ball play you.

# BODY AND STICK POSITIONING DRILL

## Purpose

Teach how to get in the correct position for making saves.

## Setup

The goalie is fully equipped and in the cage; the coach has a stick and multiple balls.

## Execution

The coach moves to various locations within a 2- to 15-yard shooting range.

## Coaching Points

Make corrections and adjustments to shooting angles, playing the pipes, and being in the ready position to make a save.

## LIVE SHOOTING DRILL

### Purpose

Bring the goalie into the phase of making saves.

### Setup

The coach prepares to shoot from various angles and distances.

### Execution

The shots begin slowly and gradually increase to full speed. The coach announces the type of shot and shot location (e.g., bounce shot to opposite hip side) in the early stages of the drill. As the progression continues, he moves in a wide arc in front of the cage to simulate shooting positions.

### Coaching Points

The goalie and coach engage in a running commentary and discussion during the drill to identify areas for improvement. Successful completion of each stage is required before increasing the speed on the shots.

# END-LINE RESTARTS AND GOALIE GROUND-BALL TECHNIQUES DRILL

## Purpose

Teach possession techniques on wide shots that go out of bounds or to the corners of the field.

## Setup

The coach has multiple balls and a player is positioned at each corner of the restraining line and offensive box area.

## Execution

The coach does not shoot the ball on the cage. Instead, he delivers the ball to the end line out of bounds or rolls the ball to the defensive corners.

## Coaching Points

The goalie works on chasing the ball once he has determined it is past the cage. He wants to gain possession by being the first and closest player to the area where the errant shot ball exited the field. He should be in a ready position when the official restarts the play. He also works on when to leave the crease area to scoop balls outside his domain and looks to move the ball up the field.

Proper goalie instruction requires a tremendous time commitment and adherence to fundamentals and daily reinforcement of skills. If possible, practice time should be set aside for goalies to work independent of the team practice.

# FACE-OFFS

Face-offs occur at the beginning of each quarter or overtime period and following each goal scored. As discussed in chapter 1, the referee supervises two opposing players matched at the face-off X. The ensuing action results in an offensive possession for one team and signals the onset of play. Winning the ground-ball war is important in winning lacrosse games. Face-off control is the equivalent of every "next ground ball" in the possession game. The face-off is not limited to the two players at the face-off X. Each team has two wing players who also play an essential role in the execution of the play.

The face-off player should line up even with the midfield line, stick in a right-handed position, his feet shoulder-width apart, and the right foot up toward the right hand closest to ball placement. The left, or back, foot should be slightly behind the right foot and serves as a push-off point for the player. The left hand should be 6 to 8 inches from the right hand before the whistle. The stance should be balanced in an athletic position, and the player should be ready to react. Instructions from the official before he blows the whistle are the commands down followed by slight pause and then set. He then blows the whistle. The face-off player must be ready to explode on the whistle. The level of concentration and anticipation before the whistle is important for success. This is a specialized area in lacrosse and requires adjusting to your opponent and flexibility in matching styles that will counter certain moves. In the quest to win the ground-ball battles, face-offs can be seen as the first or next ground ball in each game situation.

All face-off drills can be done at various speeds and progress to live full-speed action.

# CLAMP-STRENGTH MOVE DRILL

## Purpose

Teach the technique of the most popular face-off strategy.

## Setup

Opposing players simulate the face-off action in a competitive setting.

## Execution

Approach the face-off X with square shoulders, establish a low center of gravity, distribute weight equally, place the right hand palm up over the ball, and place the left hand palm down 6 inches down the stick. On the whistle, rotate the top hand forward and attempt to clamp down on the ball with the head of the stick. Push the left hand forward to secure the ball with both hands on the stick. Use your power side (left leg and foot) to generate the initial push, while the right foot comes forward with the right hand across the head of the stick. Work to push the ball between the legs by pivoting on the right foot and screen or box out your opponent. Move quickly to scoop, cradle, and gain possession of the ball. Both players return to the ready position and play through until one of them gains possession.

## Coaching Points

Teach and reinforce concepts by varying the matchups and countermoves. Create a friendly competition and progress to 3v3 with wing play.

## RAKE-SPEED MOVE DRILL

### Purpose

Teach the advantages of a face-off technique based on quickness.

### Setup

Opposing players simulate the face-off action in a competitive setting.

### Execution

Approach the face-off X with square shoulders, establish a low center of gravity, distribute weight equally, place the right hand palm up over the ball, and place the left hand palm down 6 inches down the stick. On the whistle, use the top (right) hand in an attempt to force your stick head into your opponent's stick-head area. Push your top (right) hand forcefully while you pull with the low (left) hand. As the ball is raked out to the left side of the face-off player, step to the ball while screening or boxing out your opponent. Move quickly to scoop, cradle, and gain possession of the ball.

### Coaching Points

Emphasize quickness and stick position. The stick must be pushed to the left by pushing top hand toward the opponent and pulling the left hand to the body to move the ball down the midfield line toward the left side. Mastery of this technique requires continued repetitions.

# General Body and Stick-Positioning Techniques for Face-Off Play

The stick must be perpendicular to the ground with the inverted pocket facing the opponent's pocket. Hands are waist-width apart or closer, with the right hand palm up and the left hand palm down. Crouch with your right foot close to your right hand and your left foot as close as possible to the right foot. Your right elbow is inside your right knee and the left elbow is outside your left knee. Your elbows are as close to the ground as possible so that your arms are nearly perpendicular to the ground. When the referee starts the play by blowing the whistle, clamp down with your right hand by bringing your stick top down and over the ball while your right foot goes to the head of your stick. As the stick clamps onto the ball, your left hand stays close to the ground and pushes away from your body, and you slide your stick under your opponent's stick. You can gain possession of the ball by scooping the ball between the legs or pushing to the left or forward. Use your right foot to balance yourself, continue drop-stepping with your left foot while pivoting off the right foot. Use your body as a screen to box out your opponent and pivot out with your body. Roll the ball out and scoop it.

## UNDER OR FLIP DRILL

### Purpose

This is a countermove to use against the clamp and rake techniques.

### Setup

Opposing players simulate the face-off action in a competitive setting.

### Execution

Approach the face-off X with square shoulders, establish a low center of gravity, distribute weight equally, place the right hand palm up over the ball, and place the left hand palm down 6 inches down the stick. Let the top of the stick roll back and step out with the right foot, push forward, and go under. Flip the ball up to gain possession or push under and out to scoop, cradle, and gain possession of the ball.

# TOPPING DRILL

## Purpose

Teach how to come over the top of the ball and control the action while looking for wing-play assistance.

## Setup

Opposing players simulate the face-off action in a competitive setting.

## Execution

Approach the face-off X with square shoulders, establish a low center of gravity, distribute weight equally, place the right hand palm up over the ball, and place the left hand palm down 6 inches down the stick. On the whistle, curl the right fingers toward the wrist so the stick head is horizontal and parallel with the stick pocket facing the ground. As the stick head turns to face the ground, slide the stick over the top of the ball so the stick traps the ball with the pocket facing down toward the ground. As you maneuver the hand and stick, step with the right foot toward the top of the stick head and plant into a pivot step.

Push the ball out so it goes behind, down the side, or forward. The face-off or wing players look to scoop, cradle, and gain possession of the ball.

## Coaching Points

This is a face-off technique designed to neutralize an opponent and incorporate wing play to help in gaining possession.

## REVERSE STEP DRILL

### Purpose

Teach a technique that can be effective in changing the tempo.

### Setup

Opposing players simulate the face-off action in a competitive setting.

### Execution

Approach the face-off X with square shoulders, establish a low center of gravity, distribute weight equally, place the right hand palm up over the ball, and place the left hand palm down 6 inches down the stick. Tilt the body slightly so the left side faces the opponent and both feet point slightly toward the right sideline. The body points toward the right sideline with elbows low. On the whistle, clamp down and push out with the left hand while sliding the stick straight down the midline toward the right sideline. Step out with the left foot so your stick head slides under your opponent's stick head. Take the ball between your legs or forward toward the goal. Try to scoop, cradle, and gain possession of the ball.

During practice, players can walk through a face-off simulation without pressure so they can work on mechanics. The advantage technique is where one player has an advantage with the first move. Two players simulate a face-off to see who can gain the advantage after the first move. In the back-to-back technique players line up opposite by squatting back to back and the ball is placed between players. On the whistle, they try to box out. These drills do not require the supervision of a coach.

# TRANSITION GAME

Successful transition offense creates many scoring opportunities in lacrosse. Transition offense is defined as a full-field offense when your team is in possession of the ball. All players should be regarded as offensive and defensive players who are capable of helping your team score goals. Successful implementation of full-field offense has four parts: breakout patterns, clearing from a restart, offensive patterns, and a secondary or slow break.

Transition offense is a team plan to successfully move the ball from your defensive half of the field to attack the goal before the opposing team is prepared to play defense. The ability to create high-percentage shots should quickly translate into greater goal production. Individual players also must be able to recognize when to settle the ball and run a 6v6 team offense. Pushing the ball up the field is a risk but a necessary trade-off to increase potential scoring chances. The advantage of playing at a fast pace is helpful even in situations where the offensive team does not have a numbers advantage.

## Reasons to Play Transition Offense

Use the quick restart as soon as you gain possession of the ball after a stoppage in play. This gives the offensive team an immediate advantage. You have the ability to move quickly from defense to offense, which forces the opposing team to be aware of proper balance of offensive players to defend your transition game. This can limit their offensive scheme. Regardless of size and athleticism, pushing the ball up the field works for a wide range of athletic abilities. The reward outweighs the risks. The return in goals scored is much greater than playing settled half-field offense. Use of open-field skills, quality shots on goal, pressure on opposing defenses, and an increased tempo are significant benefits. The game is more enjoyable for athletes to play. More players are in the rotation, fundamentals and skills improve, and player and ball movement are emphasized. This reinforces the team concept, which is crucial to overall success in lacrosse. Midfielders must be able to play on both ends of the field. The return of the all-around midfielder prevents the opposing team from running players to the substitution area and keeps them on the field for long stretches of playing time. The greater emphasis on passing and catching benefits the team in other areas of lacrosse skills. Each team member has a role. Practicing transition offense is disguised conditioning. Moving the ball and getting up and down the field during practice create a better-conditioned athlete. Transition teams are stronger than opponents as the game progresses by using roster depth and playing at a fast pace. Transition offense is effective against zone defenses. Many times your offense beats the zone down the field before the opponent can set up. Basic concepts used in transition offense concerning ball movement are effective against double-team defenses and zones. Transition offenses score in spurts that can discourage opponents. If a transition team falls behind in the score, they have the ability to rally back more quickly than they could with a methodical 6v6 scheme.

Defensive personnel who are athletic become ball handlers and learn to go to the cage. The team does not need a superstar offensive player to be the focal point. Unselfish open-field players who can find openings are successful in this scheme. The defense can create transition opportunities by getting the ball to the ground and pushing up from the defensive half of the field. All players feel they are part of the offense because the transition approach builds team pride and improves chances for scoring. The second or third pass leading to a goal, the hockey assist, becomes more valued.

## Transition Concepts

The fundamentals required to play a transition style in lacrosse include the following concepts. Begin with a strategy to advance the ball up the field: If you see an open stick, throw the ball. Always hustle to create an uneven situation: You must beat your man down the field. Reinforce team offense rules: Pass and cut, move without the ball, give and go. Pass the ball up the field and fill the lanes: See the whole field. Run the traditional fast break into the secondary or transition break: Keep pushing until you are forced to go 6v6. Look away to the opposite side of the field: If the ball side is covered, swing the ball for an isolation dodge on the weak side or recut to the ball. Ball movement is essential: The ball moves quicker than you can run; do not hold the ball.

## Organization and Patterns

The following sections describe player's organization and patterns.

### Break Out From Goalie Possession

Goalies and defensemen: The goalie calls out possession to alert the defensive players that your team has the ball. Defensive players in the wing positions release to the corners of the field to spread out the riding team and force them to cover a large area. The defenseman closest to the crease area remains to protect the goalie and cover rebounds. Once the goalie has clean possession, the clearing pattern begins (see figure 12.1).

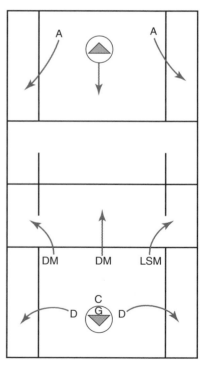

**Figure 12.1**  Break out from goalie possession.

Midfielders: If your man shoots the ball, you immediately release up the field. The option to receive the pass and run the ball out is always available. If the goalie has the ball, the two outside midfielders cover the corners and the third becomes the middle man or cutter. These midfielders break to open areas and adjust to each other's position. They must not overcrowd an area, which allows the riding team to cover the field. Outside midfielders can break to the sideline if possible; always move to an open area and call for the ball.

Attackmen: These players must move to the ball to keep them in the game. Attackmen prevent the defensemen from sliding up the field, give the midfielders a greater area to work in, and put themselves in an open area to receive the ball and begin possession in the offensive half of the field. If the player isn't moving the ball, the coach should put another player in who will. The attackmen's main responsibility is moving the ball.

The midfielder can run the ball out and create offense or, if pressured, can redirect the ball to a defenseman and clear the ball up the opposite side away from pressure. The goalie uses the full allotted time in the crease. If all midfielders are covered, the goalie can exit the crease and use the corner or wing defensemen as outlets for the initial clearing pass.

### Midfielder Cutting to the Ball

M1: Receives the pass and runs the ball out and creates a fast break or pass down the side for transition

M2, A1, A2: Get to an open area to receive the pass and create an unsettled situation

D1: Is available for a redirected pass and swings the ball back to the goalie, who clears out the backside

D2: Stays close to the crease area

D3: Is available on the backside for a redirected pass

M3, A3: Serve as primary receivers of the redirected clearing pattern

If the ball goes to a defenseman in the corner, he looks for the midfielder cutting to find the open area (see figure 12.2). Midfielders cut and replace to balance the field and create proper spacing. The far-side midfielder needs to be aware of

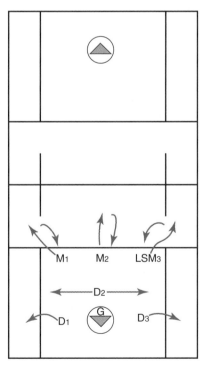

**Figure 12.2**   Midfielder cutting to the ball.

staying onside if the defenseman carries the ball over the midfield line into the offensive half of the field.

### Inbounds Clearing Pattern

Dl: Starts with the ball

Ml: Clears out the corner area

Al: Clears down to the goal line extended

M2: Cuts to open area, constant cutting based on ball location

M3: Stays onside to release Dl if he carries the ball over

D2: Stays home for transition defense if clear is unsuccessful

D3: Moves to crease area to protect the goal; can be available for redirect pass

Once the ball crosses the midfield line, the offense shifts to ball-movement positions to spread the defense and make them cover a wider area. The offense can attack the cage from five scoring positions in front of the goal.

Once the ball goes down the side by passing to the wing attack player, the remaining offensive players go to predetermined spots. The teaching point is, if you are open, the ball will find you; there is no need for you to find the ball.

When the ball is passed to a wing attack player, the opposite wing automatically cuts to the point behind the goal. The attack player makes the pass from an area that keeps the goalie from intercepting the pass. The goal line extended is a generally safe area to make the pass, depending on movement and defensive pressure. The attack player receiving the ball should be in a position that allows him to receive the pass and go either direction to feed or drive to the cage. The attack player comes down the goal line extended, fakes a front swing, and then breaks to the point (see figure 12.3).

Midfielders fill three positions to establish the offensive pattern. The top of the ball side is occupied by the midfielder who

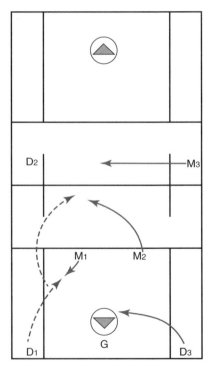

**Figure 12.3** Inbound clearing pattern.

originally carried the ball; the second midfielder looks to fill the backside position that was vacated by the attack player who went behind the goal; and the third midfielder fills the top spot on the backside. Seeing and spacing the field to identify the open areas becomes easier through practice and repetition.

## Creating Offensive Opportunities During the Transition Period

The transition pattern requires the defense to adjust quickly within the restraining line. It is advantageous to attack the goal before the opposing team gets settled into its team defensive scheme. The skill level of the offensive players is higher when they can play this style of offensive lacrosse. The secondary break provides situations that allow you to play to your strengths. These include dodging a defensive player who is moving toward the offensive player, moving the ball in a way that forces defensive players to turn their heads and lures them out of a backup position, preventing the opponent from communicating because they are adjusting to the rapid change from playing offense to defense, cutting to the ball and off the ball to create open lanes for feeds and dodges, using the wing position for feeding without pressure, and creating shots from inside 10 yards for offensive players of average ability who will convert at a higher percentage.

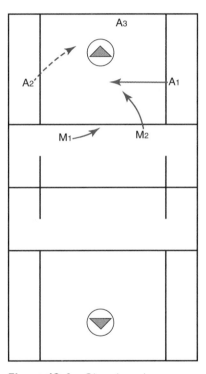

**Figure 12.4**  Slow break.

### Slow Break

During a slow break, the wing (M2) can pass to the cutter for a high-percentage shot, pass to M3 in a good dodging situation, or redirect the ball to where the cutter (Ml) relocates to the wing. The wing (M2) fills the top, and M3 slides across top to balance the field (see figure 12.4).

### Relocation

If you are unable to run the transition pattern, you can reset and settle into the 6v6 offensive pattern. This creates a settled situation.

## Active Players in Transition Offense

The emphasis during practice drills is to simulate game situations. Transition drills mimic realistic ball handling from various spots on the field. You can also run them with groups to increase game and field awareness. And they provide an opportunity to continue disguised conditioning through running while playing lacrosse.

## SCOOP AND PASS DRILL

### Purpose
Introduce the concept of defensive possession leading to transition offense.

### Setup
The goalie is positioned in the cage with defensive players in designated areas inside the defensive perimeter of 15 yards.

### Execution
Goalies work to improve ball-handling skills by simulating a game-situation outlet pass. Place the ball on the ground in the general crease area. The goalie must clamp and rake into his stick to gain clean possession, make the clearing call, and pass to a moving target.

### Coaching Points
Emphasize the 7v6 advantage of the defensive team, the importance of turning a save or turnover into a successful clearing opportunity, and the prevention of rebound or second-shot scoring chances for the opposing team.

# BREAK-OUT DRILL

## Purpose

Emphasize defensive stick handling and spacing the field when clearing the ball.

## Setup

The goalie and three defensemen are positioned in the crease area.

## Execution

This is a traditional three-man clearing drill off a simulated shot. The wing defensemen break to the corners of the field. The crease defenseman protects goal area and waits for the completed first pass, reads riding attack positions, and breaks up the field to the open area.

## Coaching Points

Just as spacing the field for offensive players is important, the same philosophy is true for advancing the ball from your defensive half of the field. The clearing team has a 7v6 advantage that can be used to create passing lanes and open areas to carry the ball over the midfield line.

# FULL-FIELD BREAKOUT DRILL

## Purpose

This drill is the final progression of the positional group transition and clearing patterns.

## Setup

The full team of three attackmen, three midfielders, three defensemen, and a goalie are positioned in a full-field scenario.

## Execution

Progress from the three-man defensive clearing breakout drill. All 10 players line up in field positions and run through all possible clearing and transition scenarios. You can run this from all potential game situations.

## Coaching Points

You can use this drill to teach all game situations. It is also useful for improving stick skills and conditioning.

## Clearing Patterns From the Defensive Half of the Field

On possession of the ball, the first look is to the midfielders or players who are up the field and have the ability to carry the ball directly to the offensive end. The 4v3 traditional fast break is preferable if you have a clear advantage. In all other situations, move the ball down the side in your transition pattern.

Transition offense is divided into three parts:

1. Initial break: This leads to the traditional 4v3 fast break. The attackman must recognize what is available and create scoring opportunities.
   a. Box
   b. Diamond
   c. X behind
2. Secondary or slow break: When the traditional 4v3 fast break is not available, use sideline options to create scoring opportunities.
   a. Ball moves from Al to A2. Ml cuts to ball. M2 can also follow and cut to ball.
   b. A2 can put ball behind and A3 finds cutter.
3. Reversal of the ball will create an open space for the offense.
   a. A2 can reverse the ball. Look for a trailer (M3 or Dl) or go isolation from up top.
   b. M3 can look for certain cutters (A3 or Ml). Move into a 1-4-1 or 2-4 offensive formation.

## Transition Situations

The spacing of defensive players to maximize clearing opportunities are described here.

1. Off shot attempt: Two defensemen and two midfielders break up the field. Crease defenseman stays close as a safety net; the third midfielder runs an under-route on the shot. Goalie outlet pass is crucial for initiating transition.
2. Turnover: Use a similar pattern based on the location of the double team or slide that gets the ball to the ground.
3. Quick or set clear: Run the clear to create a transition offense. Push the ball to the strong side of the field and then go weak side.

## DODGING AND CREATING OPEN SPACE DRILL

### Purpose

Raise the awareness of creating and using open space to create offensive opportunities.

### Setup

A player has a lacrosse stick, ball, and access to the offensive half of the field.

### Execution

The player can be creative in visualizing those areas of stick protection and fundamental stick work to simulate game conditions.

### Coaching Points

Remind players to see the field; play with their head up; move the ball; and to dodge to pass, feed, and shoot.

# DONOVAN DRILL

While attending the National Lacrosse Coaches Convention in 1984, I noted the large number of clinicians who presented on the topic of transition offense. I had lengthy conversations with two defensive coaches I have always relied on through the many years for their insights and expertise. Bob Shillinglaw (University of Delaware) and Dave Slafkosky (United States Military Academy and University of Maryland) agreed that a presentation on transition defense was long overdue. I presented a transition drill at the following year's convention in Philadelphia. While coaching at the C.W. Post campus of Long Island University, we called the drill full-field transition. Jack Kaley introduced it as the Donovan drill in his practices that spring.

## Purpose

This drill teaches and highlights all settled and unsettled situations that can occur during a lacrosse game. It also is a disguised conditioning drill because of the number of times the ball goes up and down the field. The coach introduces each progression as play develops in sequence. Players learn to identify whether the numbers are even, they have an offensive advantage, or they are playing at a defensive disadvantage.

## Setup

Divide the team into two equal groups. The teams each have three attack players, three defensemen, and a goalie on its end of the field within the box area. Player positions are the same as before the face-off in a game. All midfielders report to the substitution box on their defensive half of the field. The coach is at the face-off X with at least a dozen balls. Each goal should also contain a dozen balls.

## Execution

The coach rolls the ball out to a midfielder entering the field of play from the box area to begin the drill with a traditional 4v3 fast break. The opposing midfielder remains on his side of the box area ready to enter the field of play in his defensive half by moving toward the ball after a save, turnover, ball out of bounds, or goal. Any defensive teammate can pass the ball to the player at the box area. This creates a 4v4 opportunity going in the opposite direction. The sequence of play continues with the progression of 5v4, 5v5, 6v5, and a concluding 6v6 (see figure 12.5).

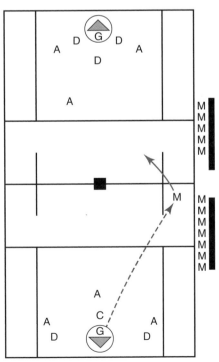

**Figure 12.5**   Donovan drill.

## Coaching Points

- Teaching points for the team on offense (with even numbers) are pass and cut and move without the ball. A numbers advantage should create a sense of urgency to attack the goal and create offense. Reinforce the teaching concepts for the fast and slow break.

- Teaching points for the team on defense (with even numbers) are to match up by identifying a player to guard. A numbers disadvantage should create a zone concept to force the offense to take an outside or low-percentage shot. Throughout the drill, stress identifying the numbers advantage and communication.

Once the drill is completed, the advantage rotates in the next cycle. This provides the opportunity for all players to play with and without the numbers advantage. Emphasize conditioning and playing at full speed. Role reversal is strongly suggested and can be accomplished by rotating all positions (attack, midfield, defense) in the substitution-box area and on the field of play. This also creates a high level of energy.

Special situations can occur at any time during a game. Review of these situations is a valuable tool when designing a practice plan. Because lacrosse is a free-flowing game, players who can recognize these situations will have a competitive advantage.

We have written this book to introduce, teach, and reinforce the concepts of lacrosse. Individual skills should follow a progression to provide the reader with a basic understanding of the skill set needed to develop proficiency in this wonderful sport. We hope that our passion for lacrosse comes through in this book. Readers should always be mindful of three things: Remember to have fun, play hard, and be positive. We welcome you to the lacrosse community and wish you success and enjoyment in our sport.

# About the Authors

**Jack B. Kaley** is the all-time leader in winning percentage (84%) for Division I and II universities and has been the head coach for the German national lacrosse team since 2009. His record of 185-33 at the New York Institute of Technology (NYIT) occurred at an academic institution that had discontinued men's lacrosse in 1978. His efforts in recruiting student-athletes to a commuter school as a part-time coach with limited resources showed positive results in the 1993 inaugural season with a No. 5 national ranking followed by an undefeated regular season in 1994, which culminated in the first of six National Championship appearances. This launched a 17-year run of excellence, which included four National Championships, a record four-time recognition as National Coach of the Year, and 75 All-American selections. Kaley amassed a 507-176 record while coaching Lynbrook High School, East Meadow High School, Long Island Lacrosse Club, Hampstead Lacrosse Club, and the German National Team. He lives in Westbury, New York.

**Rich Donovan** is an assistant coach for the German National Lacrosse Team; the boys' lacrosse coach at The Wheatley School in Long Island, New York; and an official with the Nassau County Lacrosse Officials Association. He began his career in lacrosse at East Meadow High School in New York and then played for the University of Massachusetts (1975-78), where he was a team captain, four-year varsity starter and letter winner on a team that enjoyed two NCAA tournament appearances. He began his coaching career at the University of Massachusetts in 1979 and had subsequent coaching jobs at CW Post College from 1983 to 1985, Hofstra University from 1986 to 1995, and several high schools in Long Island from 1980 to 1982 and from 1996 to the present, and Bridgeport Barrage (Major Lacrosse League) in 2002. Rich lives in East Meadow, New York.